Miracles Blossom
from The Spirit Within

Frances Purnell-Dampier

Order this book online at www.trafford.com
or email orders@trafford.com

Most Trafford titles are also available at major online book retailers.

Illustrated by Shelley Capovilla

Printed in the United States of America.

ISBN: 978-1-4669-8021-1 (sc)
ISBN: 978-1-4669-8020-4 (hc)
ISBN: 978-1-4669-8019-8 (e)

Library of Congress Control Number: 2013905120

Trafford rev. 03/18/2013

 www.trafford.com

North America & international
toll-free: 1 888 232 4444 (USA & Canada)
phone: 250 383 6864 ♦ fax: 812 355 4082

Dedication

This book is dedicated to my three wonderful sons Charles, Trevis, and Desmond. I love them very much. They are God's precious gifts to me. Also, I thank my gorgeous daughters-in-law Minna and Maureen, who are the best mothers ever for my beautiful grandchildren.

To my seven lovely granchildren, Jenee, Tiana, Royale, TJ, Christion, Deion, Jasmine, and my two grandchildren by marriage, Jonea and Monay; they are the love of my life.

To my sister, Deloris, for her unwavering love, support, and inspiration, and my oldest sister, Elizabeth, who is a great role model. Thanks for always being there for me.

To my mother, Hazel Hobbs-Purnell Walker, who taught me to be morally centered, and to my stepfather, Rev. W. W. Walker, who provided spiritual guidance to me and my sisters.

Additionally, thanks to all of my friends who contributed and poured out their heartfelt stories for this book so that others would find comfort, inspiration, and courage. These are the everyday people whom God spoke about. I call them *disciples of Christ.*

Contents

Morning Daily Prayer

Father, thank you for another day
I thank you more than words can say
Open my eyes wide and clear
To see the miracles that other's fear.
Prepare my mind to receive
Ways to help others to believe
In you Heavenly Father
Amen

By Frances Purnell-Dampier

Introduction

Today is a good day for a miracle. Each day I wake up with eager anticipation of a glorious, miraculous day that God has made for me. I bounce out of bed and throw on my warm, comfy robe and slippers and head downstairs. As I get to the stairs' landing, I automatically open the blinds to the outside world. Opening the blinds, I expect as usual a beautiful, spectacular landscape of blue skies, bright rays from the glistening sun, white billowing clouds, and sometimes a breathtaking colorful monarch butterfly floating effortless by the windowpane.

Other days, the landscape paints a different view and the colors hold a variety of wonderful hues. Heavy raindrops soak the earth, dark grey or black clouds cover the sky. I hear the whistling of the wind, the roll of thunder and the bright striking force of lightning. No matter what kind of day it is, I marvel at God's handiwork! These phenomena cause me to reflect on just how grand and magnificent God is!

Settling in with my hot, steaming coffee, I rejoice in God's goodness. The awesome fact that God woke me up and gave me eyes to see, ears to hear, a mind to think, a voice to speak, and a heart to love is more than a miracle but a remarkable blessing in itself. To think that God thinks of us each second, each minute, each hour, each day is incredible and mind blowing! In fact, God thought of us before we were conceived. Months ago, God revealed a poem to me about this very thing.

Poem: The Soul

I've wondered long and hard
About this thing called "The Soul"
It seems it has some magic
Which makes the body whole?

I imagine God sitting there
In Heaven on his throne
Fashioning each and every one
As if it were his own.

Making sure that each of them
Were special in their own way
Giving each a unique gift
To use from day to day.

I see a loving God holding it
So gently in his hands
Stroking it with tenderness
Knowing exactly where it will land.

As God surveys the women
He spots the parent to be
Ah-ha, he thinks to himself
I'll plant you inside "she"

The Soul nestles in the baby
All snug warm and cozy
Until that glorious day
When it comes out wet and rosy

Throughout the years the Soul
Computes every life detail
Transmitting them to God
Who keeps a lasting trail.

Then when life's journey finally ends
And our time on Earth is done
God beckons for the Soul to come
Back to his Father's arms.

By Frances Purnell-Dampier

We tend to take his miracles for granted. Sometimes when I am deeply in thought about God's gifts and grace, I think about a song I heard as a child. The song went like this.

Said the night wind to the little lamb,

"Do you see what I see?"

Said the little lamb to the shepherd boy,

"Do you hear what I hear?"

Said the shepherd boy to the mighty king,

"Do you know what I know?

I constantly pray for God to show me miracles and he constantly provides them for me, but he also provides them for each of us on this earth. When I observe a miracle, I immediately shout it out. Other people look at me with skepticism. I think, what can be done to help others see that when they were saved from an automobile crash and they heard a voice in their ear telling them to slow down as a speeding car dashed before their eyes, that the voice was none other than a "God Whisper"? Why don't they know and recognize the miracle when they are stressed out because they have a major bill to pay but not enough money coming in but "unexpectedly" when they go to the mailbox there is a check from someone for the exact amount they needed for the bill?

These occurrences happen daily. Some people call them coincidences. They are small miracles from God. As an answer to my question about how to get people to understand about these everyday miracles, God prepared an answer during my recent trip to Paris, France.

Spirit Within

Jesus loves you
Each and everyday
In such a very special way
He's there in everything you do
Trust in HIM and you'll get through.

Before he left this earthly place
He told his disciples what he must face
A horrible death upon the cross
An inconceivable spiritual loss.

But death was not the ultimate goal
It was salvation for our lost soul
He left the HOLY SPIRIT to guide us
To be a Comforter and one we'd trust
Oh, Father, Son, Holy Spirit, we rejoice
And thank you for making us your loving choice.

By Frances Purnell-Dampier

Chapter 1

Paris Trip: God Reveals Miracle Plan

At last, forty years later I finally embarked on my trip to Paris, a dream of a lifetime. I took French in high school and college anticipating a trip to Paris in the near future, but as life, marriage, career, and children would have it, the dream of Paris was placed on the backburner. Now, after retirement, the dream was finally realized. The all-inclusive eight-day cruise was going to be unbelievable. A tour guide was given the task of escorting us on a daily excursion to the city of Paris and surrounding notable areas. It was a miraculous adventure witnessing the Champs-Élysées and the glorious sights along the Seine River. Along this boulevard was the world capital of exquisite shopping! The finest luxury designer brands lined the street with famous stores like Chanel, Dior, and Azzaro. This was a fashionista's dream.

Drifting along the Seine on our ship, we were able to view the sheer beauty of monuments indicative of the Industrial Age, all stately standing in glory, such as the Petit Palais, the Grand Palais, the Eiffel Tower, the Notre Dame Cathedral, the Conciergerie, and the gigantic palace of the Louvre. Strolling down the streets of Paris smelling and tasting the mouthwatering buttery croissants with hot ham and cheese oozing out of it, dribbling down the corners of my mouth and later biting into the warm, sweet, flaky crepes made me realize that all was right with the world.

Visiting historical sites like Auvers-sur-Oise where Van Gogh painted over fifty masterpieces and later died of alcoholism and manic depression, gave me insight into some of his most famous work. Exciting as well was visiting the city of Rouen, where breathtaking cathedrals displayed master craftsmanship of biblical images and carvings on the wall and windows. This city was also famous for being the place where Joan of Arc was burned at the stake for expressing that she had heard a "God Whisper" telling her to take back France from England. Because she had faith and listened to God, people called her a witch and burned her at the stake. Seeing her gravesite and statue was a testimony of her strong belief in God. Doing God's will is not always easy. Another memorable sight was seeing the D-Day beaches, museum, and memorial for the 9,000 soldiers still buried there. This sight, with an array of white crosses with a backdrop of soldiers' names inscribed along the walls, caused my heart to stand still and I became awestruck, inspired, and extremely grateful for their great service to our country.

Thinking God had given me the miracle of a lifetime with my Paris trip made my heart sing praises, but to my amazement that was not the reason for my trip to Paris. God had something else entirely different in mind for me, a commandment/mission that left me speechless and awe-inspired.

It all began when our tour guide asked us if we wanted her to show us how to use the Metro, Paris' train. Three new friends that I had formed a close bond with on the tour and I quickly raised our hands along with some other people. We had seen earlier on the tour bus an entire street of flea markets with souvenir shops and all kinds of delicious tasty foods. We couldn't wait to get there. Taking the train was scary, so I wrote meticulous notes while the guide told us which streets to look for and which transfer to take to get to the flea market. We spent the day shopping, eating, laughing, trying on berets and literally just enjoying the day until suddenly it started pouring rain. Immediately, we ran back to the metro station. Soaking wet and cold, I pulled out my wet directions on how to navigate our way back through the train maze and figure out the transfer back to the ship. As we were walking through the Metro, two other people, Laura and Katlyn, who looked very lost, from our Viking tour were also trying to figure their way out of the maze. Although we had never officially met, we noticed their Viking badges right away; therefore, we joined forces, determined that we would figure it out together. One of them, Laura seemed drawn to me right away, and as we walked and searched for the next street sign, she instantly began telling me that she was so happy to be in Paris and that she just had to make the journey to Paris because her doctor had given her only six months to live. She had been diagnosed with pancreatic cancer and she was searching for answers. Startled by her admission, I blurted out that I believed in miracles. I didn't want to give her false hope, so I continued by saying that God would show her the direction to take and that he would guide her no matter what the outcome. I told her to trust in God and listen for answers from the Holy Spirit. That day we bonded and became friends throughout the trip. Laura, Katlyn, Ethel, and their husbands, Jonathan, Sal, and Derrick, plus Denise and her mother began eating together every night and bonding on our various tour trips. We talked about everything and had so many wonderful laughs. We found out that Katlyn and Sam were going to get married on the ship and we all put our heads together to help plan it and make it a joyous occasion. What fun we were having!

After one of our delicious dinners, I went seeking the program director, Sam. I asked him if he could find out where the Lady of Lourdes' city was because I knew it was in France. I informed him that six or seven of us wanted to take a side trip there. I also told him that I had met this beautiful young lady who said she only had six months to live and I knew people took pilgrimages to the city of Lourdes because the water was said to have miraculous powers and could cure illnesses. The program director, Sam, researched and finally told me that we couldn't go there because it was five hundred miles away. I blurted out to Sam, "I don't understand why God put this idea in my head. I thought this was going to be a miracle for Laura." Sam looked up at me and uttered with certainty, "I don't believe in miracles!" My eyes widened, and without thinking, I said, "What? Well, Sam, just wait until the end of the week. God's going to show you some miracles. Mark my word." Why I said that, I don't have a clue, and I was puzzled myself as to why I even thought of the city of Lourdes. Usually, I consider those thoughts to be associated with "God Whispers."

After the most fabulous three-course meal, I decided to turn in for the night. Settling into a relaxing slumber, with the waves crashing against the ship and rocking me ever so gently, I felt a presence. The voice felt comforting, soothing, and very familiar. Fortunately, I had encountered this voice a few times now and I immediately knew that it was God. Like a father speaking to his loving child, he began what I call his "God Whisper." Like twice before, he spoke telepathically. I understood everything he said, and I in return spoke to him telepathically. Immediately, I was witnessing a CinemaScopelike vision of me talking to Sam earlier in the day. It was as if the replay button had been hit and I was an outside observer watching Sam and I engaged in the conversation we had experienced earlier. I watched Sam tell me again that he didn't believe in miracles and watched me tell him to just wait until the end of the week. As that vision diminished, I heard God's voice beckoning me to his urgent words, "People like Sam do not recognize that I perform miracles for them every day, both big and small. These miracles and signs are my kisses to them to let them know that I love them and am there for them. They think miracles have to be huge like the parting of the Red Sea, Jericho, Daniel, Lazarus. No, no! I perform miracles all the time!" Suddenly, in a flash, I saw the outline of a book. God began, like a magnificent artist painting on a canvas, directing, if you will, the contents of each half of a book. Pointing to the left side of the book, he said, "Tell them what miracles are and how they are to recognize them. Collect miracles from everyday people, telling their stories so that their stories can become testimonies of how much I love them." He waved his right hand over the second part of the book. His voice was like a teacher's explaining a lesson to a student. "I want them to keep a journal of their miracles so they can look back at them and gain inspiration when they feel lonely and know that I was there with them every step of the way." He gave me specific directions for the journal, which I will reveal in a later chapter. He then whispered softly two times, **"Spirit within. Spirit within."** Telepathically, I somehow knew that God had given me the title of the book, but my humanness invoked me to ask him what *Spirit*

Within had to do with miracles. I inquired, "Lord, do you want me to put a subtitle about miracles?" God lovingly whispered, "Remember the Trinity: the Father, Son, and Holy Spirit." His voice trailed off and I fell back into a deep slumber until my alarm went off. I didn't have a lot of time before breakfast, so I quickly scribbled the conversation as best as I could remember it. Usually when I am at home I keep a pad by my bed, and when I have these "God Whispers" I either write something down quickly on the pad or run downstairs to write it down before I forgot. Who would think that God would intervene during my vacation in Paris? Oh, he does have a sense of humor though. As quickly as I could get dressed, I found my new friends and could hardly contain myself, telling them about my revelation. They didn't act startled by my story at all but encouraged me to write the next book, but I argued that I had no intention of writing another book. They brought me back to reality by saying, "You're the one who believes in miracles. Now God has given you a mission. Are you going to do it or not?" Without hesitation, I replied, "Well, I guess I'm writing another book on miracles."

Later that day, they had someone come in and tell Christmas stories in the lounge. Denise and her mother decided to go, but I decided I'd better go back to the room and try to contact my family with my new tablet to let them know that I was safe. After

I finally got the message sent and scribbled down the events in my journal with more details of the sights I had seen the previous day, I went to the lounge to find Denise and her mother. When I spotted Denise, her eyes were like a little child's opening Christmas presents. She was babbling about finding a pickle. I stopped her and said, "Slow down and tell me the whole story." Apparently, the storyteller told them a German classic fairytale about these children who were left alone and all they could find to eat were pickles. These pickles saved the children's lives and they lived happy ever after. (Personally, I would call this a miracle.) This story became a tradition and was told from one generation to another. To honor the classic fairytale, every Christmas a pickle is hidden in the Christmas tree. Whoever finds it receives a special gift. So Denise excitedly said, "Guess what? I found the pickle. Everyone was looking in the tree, but I decided to go ask the receptionist if it could be somewhere other than the tree." The receptionist told Denise, "I don't know!" Denise took that as a clue that perhaps it was somewhere else. She started looking all around the receptionist's desk, and to her surprise she found it inside a huge vase on the reception counter. Happily, she took the pickle to Sam, the program director, and received a set of Parisian stationery. At that moment, Sam interrupted because it was six thirty. We always met in the lounge so that Sam could give us a rundown of the next day's itinerary. Then as usual, he asked someone in the audience with pure hands to pull for a prize, one prize per night. All cabin numbers were placed in the basket. Someone from the audience volunteered and pulled the number. "Number 211," she called. Wow! That was Denise's cabin number. Denise shouted, "That's my number. I've won twice today!" She accepted the gift and looked at Sam. "Twice today, Sam!" He nodded in acknowledgement.

Sam continued by saying that they were going to have a big drawing after dinner that night and that the receptionist had tickets to sell for those who wanted to purchase them. Denise, her mom, and I left the lounge to go back to the room to change for dinner. About an hour later, I returned to the formal dining room and found Denise, her mom, and two more people sitting with them. Denise smiled, patted the chair next to her, and said, "We saved you a seat!" I said, "You all are so sweet. Thank you for thinking of me." The couple said, "Are you all traveling together?" We all blurted out that we just met at the airport and became instant friends. Everyone thought we had known each other all our lives. I considered it to be a miracle to find such generous, friendly people, because I was traveling alone. God had placed them in my life at just the right moment. Denise's voice jolted me back to reality. "Have you bought your tickets yet?"

"To what?" I asked. "The raffle tickets to the big draw after dinner tonight. I already bought three for ten euros and I'm going to win. I know I'm going to win. I already won twice. I just feel it," Denise exclaimed. Then she pointed to the couple and asked them if they were going to buy tickets and the man said no way was he going to waste money when Denise was so sure of herself. Well, that didn't stop me, because I believed in miracles, so I figured I at least had a chance. I excused myself and hurried off to purchase my three tickets. On the way back to the table, Denise was running past me, saying she was buying three more tickets for her mother. Boy, was she caught up in the excitement.

After dinner, we all went to the lounge. Laura joined us at the table and we all huddled with eager anticipation. Sam began by telling us that it was time for the draw and everyone needed to get their tickets out. As usual, he asked who had pure hands to draw the number. Laura's hands went up and she shouted, "Me!" Sam told her to come on up. She bounced up from her seat with joy. Sam's helper mixed up the numbers and just as Laura was putting her hands in the basket, Denise blurted, "Two-one-one." Out came Laura's hands and in disbelief, she screamed," Two-one-one." Sam's helper looked at the number again and said, "Yes, it is 211." Denise was in shock herself and went to collect her gift. She said to Sam, "Three prizes today!" Sam nodded. Denise was remembering what I had told her about Sam not believing in miracles. By that time, Denise was becoming a convert herself. When she returned to her seat, she asked me, "What's going on? This is weird. Am I psychic?" I said, "No, it's just your time." Two other numbers were called and then Laura pulled number 211 again! Denise was beside herself when she went up. She started apologizing to folks, saying the number was not hers but her mothers. When she returned to her seat, I saw her eyes tearing up. She was in a mesmerized state. I said, "We had better not win any more or these people are going to throw daggers at us. I'm not going to even think of my number." But the girl showing the prizes pulled out this huge jar of shower gel. It was the same one as the miniature they had in our rooms and I loved the silky feeling it gave you as the lather seemed to multiply all over the body. Without hesitation or thought, I blurted out, "I want that." I watched Laura pull out the number and blurt out in total disbelief, "Two-three-three," my room number. "Oh no!" I stammered. "I didn't mean to think it," I said to Denise. I stumbled up to get the gift and felt piercing eyes from the crowd. Denise and I were both in tears by then because we felt a supernatural presence. We just stared at each other, and then I heard Laura's voice again, "Number 233." I felt faint; this couldn't be happening. I gathered myself together, and with my heart beating rapidly, I gained enough strength to get my gift. With tears in my eyes, I looked up at Sam. He threw up his hands as if to say, "I give up." I took that to mean he was caught up too in this supernatural moment. I found out later when I was more composed that I had won the DVD of all the spectacular places we were visiting on the ship. This was the DVD that everyone admired as it played daily on the receptionist desk. It was an absolute treasure.

After the draw, the captain came up to speak. He told everyone the unexpected news to the other passengers, "You are going to witness something that we have never had on this ship before in a few minutes." And suddenly the music began and Katlyn and Sal came strolling down the aisle with Katlyn looking beautiful with a white retro outfit and veil and Sal in his dapper black suit. To make this even more special, Laura performed the ceremony. Passengers were shocked but pleasantly surprised—another miracle for everyone. The wedding was so special.

The next morning, as I was going to breakfast I saw Sam. I looked at him and he looked at me. I said, "Now, Sam, do you believe in miracles?" Sam said, "A little bit more." That's all God needs, a crack in a doubter's heart, because then there's room for so many other miracles to fill his heart.

The night before we were to leave Paris, I spotted Laura in the reading section. She had been feeling very ill one of the days and we were all quite concerned. I went over to check on her. When she saw me, she grabbed both my hands. She said God had given her a revelation that everything was going to be all right. She said before she was worried about dying and rather scared but she was not afraid anymore. God had given her peace with whatever was to happen with her. Because we were in a public place she said, "Can you say a silent prayer with me?" And we did, with our eyes closed and heads bowed. At that very moment, God spoke to me, and I said, "Come with me to my cabin. I have something to give you." We entered my room and I reached for the bag of souvenirs I had bought to take home. Without hesitation, I unwrapped this beautiful white angel that I had bought for myself because I collect angels, and I gave it to her. She said, "No, I cannot accept it because you bought it for yourself." "I thought I was buying it for myself, but when we prayed together God whispered to me to give it to you as a gift from him. He wants you to know that he is with you and will take care of you." We hugged, not knowing if we would ever see each other again but knowing that God had put us in each other's lives for a reason. As 2 Corinthians 13:14 says, "May the grace of the Lord Jesus, and the love of God, and the fellowship of the Holy Spirit be with you all."

When I think of God's Miracles, I think of…
(Poem)

Glittering unearthed diamonds
Crystal shimmering lakes
Cascading aromatherapy oil messages
Crying newborn babies
Lush green rainforests
Twinkling shooting stars
Radiant yellow sun rays
Chirping blue birds
Swaying yellow daffodils
Flittering multicolored butterflies
Crashing stormy seas
Bold, striking sunsets
Crimson red roses
Silky, smooth white gardenia petals
Scintillating, bright stars
Iridescent, colorful rainbows
Snowcapped mountains
Mighty majestic eagles
Fresh honeysuckle summer's air
Pure white driven snow
Intense blue skies
Dancing field of swaying flowers
Thirsty humans seeking wisdom
Unseen angels, spirits and beloved departed souls.

By Frances Purnell-Dampier

Chapter 2

What are Miracles?

The Holy Bible tells us that a miracle is an unusual happening, one that goes against logic or the normal laws of nature. Miracles are done by the power of God.

Many philosophers and creative thinkers have attempted to answer that question.

Henry Thoreau quoted, **"Could a greater miracle take place than for us to look through each other's eyes for an instant."**

Bernard Berenson quoted, **"Miracles happen to those who believe in them."**

Mother Teresa quoted, **"I prefer you to make mistakes in kindness than work miracles in unkindness."**

Saint Augustine quoted, **"Miracles are not contrary to nature, but only contrary to what we know about nature."**

An anonymous quotes states, **"Miracles are natural. When they do not occur, something has gone wrong."**

Miracles are natural, and thanks to God Almighty they still are happening. The only thing that has gone wrong is our ability to recognize and understand when they occur with us. Have you ever experienced something extraordinary and so implausible and unbelievable that goes against what you know as real and sane? When the event occurred, did you scratch your head in disbelief? Did you toss the event aside as if to say it was impossible and therefore I will pretend it never happened so that people will not consider me crazy or foolish? Have you ever felt a presence and looked around to find nothing there and think, now that's strange. Have you ever been on your way somewhere and a voice in your head said to go back home and once you returned home you noticed that you left the coffee pot on? Did you tell someone about it but instead of saying a voice inside your head told you to turn around and go back, you said, "Something told me to turn around!" Well, that voice was God, Jesus, the Holy Spirit. All of these occurrences are miracles performed by God, Jesus, or the Holy Spirit.

Are you struggling in your belief in miracles? One of my favorite quotes states, **"Faith is not believing God can, it is knowing he will."**

When in doubt, there are several things one must do.

Six Strategies for Attracting Miracles

1. Be open to all possibilities.

2. Allow yourself to experience a spiritual awakening.

3. Pray and call on God for guidance and assurances.

4. Draw positive energy into your life. Weed out negativity.

5. Expect a miracle to happen in all circumstances.

6. Make time to meditate daily to attract all that is good and holy.

A more detailed analysis of these strategies will occur in chapter 4.

A Christian should have no trouble believing in miracles because the very word *Christian* means to be Christlike, to be of Christ. The Bible tells us that if we are united in Christ, we are transformed. We are reborn a new creature. The key word is *reborn*. Just as a newborn baby is not fearful of anything, we must also be free to believe and step out on faith in our willingness to experience all that God has to offer. Know that we are new creatures in God and our power is limitless because we are indeed

children of the Most High. A favorite mentor, Maya Angelou, once said, **"Stand up straight and realize who you are, that you tower over your circumstances. You are a child of God. Stand up straight."**

Growing up, most Christians have learned about miracles in Sunday School, Bible study, or from the pastor during regular services when he preaches different sermons. The stories in the Old Testament have always been fascinating. The New Testament is even more intriguing, with Jesus arriving on the scene. Jesus actually walked among us and witnessed firsthand the humanness of each of us. He loved everybody no matter what their station was in life; no matter if they were Jews or Gentiles, no matter what their affliction happened to be. He performed miracles to all who were present believers and nonbelievers. God certainly did us a favor when he performed a most perfect miracle and placed Jesus Christ in the womb of our Virgin Mary. Without that miracle, we would undoubtedly all be condemned to a life of eternal sin.

As Christians, when we testify of God's grace and miracles, we honor his name. Sharing miracle stories with others puts a smile, no doubt, on God's face—probably as illuminating as one million times the sun's rays. Three of God's most powerful stories in the Bible explain Jesus' healing and miraculous capabilities.

One such powerful miracle in the Bible comes from the book of John, chapter 2. Jesus was at a wedding with his mother. When the wine was all gone, his mother, Mary, went to Jesus and told him that all of the wine was gone. Jesus looked at his mother and replied, **"Dear woman, why do you involve me? My time has not yet come."** But because Jesus was an obedient son, he told the servants to bring all the available jars. They brought six stone water jars that held from twenty to thirty gallons each. Jesus directed them to fill the jars with water. Then he said, **"Now draw some of it out and take it to the master of the banquet."** The servants obediently did as they were told and when the master tasted it, the water turned into the most delicious wine the master had ever tasted. In fact, he remarked that someone had been holding out on him. This was the first of Jesus' miraculous signs that he performed at Cana. He thus revealed his glory, and the disciples in Galilee began to put unyielding faith in him.

John 4:43-54 tells us of a moving story of one of these heartwarming miracles. This second story explains that Jesus was visiting Cana in Galilee, where he had performed miracles before. The Galileans knew of his miracles and the word of what he was capable of doing in terms of healing was known all over the region. An official in Capernaum heard that Jesus was in Galilee and went to him and begged Jesus to come with him in order to heal his son, who was very ill. The worried father was insistent that Jesus honor his request because he feared his son was near death. Interestingly, Jesus said to him, **"Unless you people see miraculous signs and wonders, you will never believe."**

The official wasn't necessarily focusing on what Jesus was trying to tell him because he had his son on his mind. Jesus no doubt shocked him when he told him to go back to Capernaum. Jesus declared to him, **"You may go. Your son will live!"** The scriptures say the man took Jesus at his word and headed back to Capernaum, which was about twenty miles from Galilee. While the man was on his way back home, his servants met him with the news that his son was alive and doing well. The royal official asked the servants if they could tell him what time the boy began getting better. The servant replied, "The fever left him yesterday at the seventh hour." The father was shocked because he realized that this was the exact time in which Jesus had said to him, "Your son will live!" Therefore, the Bible tells us that the royal official and everyone in his household believed in Jesus and the power of his miracles.

This third story comes from John, chapter 4. Jesus had left Judea and was on his way back to Galilee. On his way back, he decided to go through Samaria because he and his disciples were thirsty and he knew Jacob had a well there. The disciples left him and went into the city for supplies. Jesus was sitting alone near the well when a Samaritan woman came to draw water. Jesus said to her, "Will you give me a drink?" The Samaritan woman was shocked that Jesus would be associating or talking to her, let alone asking her to draw him some water. The woman said to Jesus, "You are a Jew and I am a Samaritan woman. How can you ask me for a drink?" In those days, Jews and Samaritans did not associate. Jesus answered her, **"If you knew the gift of God and who it is that asks you for a drink, you would have asked him and he would have given you living water."** The woman was confused about this living water Jesus spoke of but Jesus continued to speak to her. He revealed that she had been married five times and that the man she was living with presently was not her husband. This woman knew immediately that she was in the midst of a prophet. Jesus spoke to her about Christ and how he was going to come back one day and take back true Christians to heaven with him. Jesus said to her, **"God is spirit, and his worshipers must worship in spirit and in truth."** And his last words to her were, "I who speak to you am he." This Samaritan woman became a true believer and went back to town to tell everyone about her encounter with Jesus. Because of her testimony, many people in town were converted and became true believers.

These three stories teach us the true meaning of why it is necessary to reveal how Jesus has intervened in our everyday lives today to perform miracles. Jesus doesn't necessarily want to have to perform miracles in order to convert us but as he said to the royal official, **"Unless you people see miraculous signs and wonders, you will never believe."** It then becomes imperative to recognize and exclaim to those who have doubt that Jesus is who he says he is and that he is our savior and our salvation. Jesus will not reveal himself to us unless we open our hearts to his infinite possibilities. Our five senses are not enough to understand the infinite degree of all that God is. It is important, therefore, to remember the recipes for attracting miracles as described earlier in the chapter. If we allow ourselves to listen to the Holy Spirit within us, then we will experience God's miracles and all that God has in store for us.

Miracles of Jesus
(Holy Bible: New International Version)

Healing of Individuals
1. Man with leprosy: Matthew 8:1-4
2. Roman centurion's servant: Matthew 8:5-13
3. Peter's mother-in-law: Matthew 8:14-15

4. Two men possessed with devils: Mark 5:1-15

5. Man with palsy: Luke 5:18-26

6. Woman with bleeding: Matthew 9:20-22

7. Two blind men: Matthew 9:27-31

8. Dumb, devil-possessed man: Matthew 9:32-33

9. Canaanite woman's daughter: Mark 7:24-30

10. Boy with devil: Luke 9:38-43

11. Devil-possessed man in synagogue: Mark 1:21-26

12. Blind man at Bethsaida: Mark 8:22-26

13. Crippled woman: Luke 13:10-17

14. Man with dropsy: Luke 14:1-4

15. Ten men with leprosy: Luke 17:11-19

16. Nobleman's son at Capernaum: John 4:46-54

17. Man born blind: John 9:1-41

Control of Nature

1. Calming the storm: Mark 4:37-41

2. Feeding of 5,000: Matthew 14:14-21

3. Walking on water: John 6:16-21

4. Fig tree withers: Mark 11:12-14

5. Huge catch of fish: Luke 5:411

6. Water into wine: John 2:1-11

Raising the Dead

1. Jairus' daughter: Luke 8:40-56

2. Widow at Nain's son: Luke 7:11-17

3. Lazarus: John 11:1-44

Chapter 3

What Role does the Holy Spirit Play in Miracles?

John 16:3

"But when he, the Spirit of Truth, comes, he will guide you into all truth. He will not speak on his own; he will speak only what he hears, and he will tell you what is yet to come."

Before writing this chapter on what role the Holy Spirit plays in miracles, I meditated and prayed to the Holy Spirit to enlighten me and to guide me to the essence of truth. It was essential to hear exactly what he wanted me to impart about God's truth. In order for me to speak God's word and grow spiritually in Christ, it was necessary to differentiate my thinking from that of the Holy Spirit. In other words, I had to evolve to a self-realization and examination of myself. Once I felt validated and cemented in my own beliefs, then I felt ready to inform others of God's infinite truths.

When I had my revelation in Paris or my "God Whisper," the last words the Holy Spirit spoke to me was, **"Remember the Trinity!"** Those words echoed in my head and saturated my brain until the thirst for more knowledge about the Holy Spirit consumed me. Meticulously, I scoured the Bible extensively, digesting every morsel of information about the Trinity. Meditating intently on God's words, my findings were these. First, the Trinity means three: God the Father, Son (Jesus), and the Holy Spirit. Although we speak of them separately at times, they are one. The Bible teaches that God speaks to Jesus and Jesus speaks to the Holy Spirit. They are of one accord. They speak the truth, God's truth. The Bible further states that no one can come to the Father except through the Son, Jesus. Then where does the Holy Spirit fit into all of this?

Remember, right before Jesus was crucified, he realized that he was going to have to leave his disciples alone. He kept telling his disciples that he was going away, but they were not ready or did not have the capacity to understand the grander plan of what Jesus was telling them. On one such occasion Jesus spoke to his disciples about this very thing. John 16:7 explains it well, **"But I tell you the truth: It is for your good that I am going away; the counselor (Holy Spirit) will not come to you; but if I go, I will send him to you."** Those are the magic words we need to remember. Jesus had to die not only to save us but also to leave us with a guiding force in our lives. When we need assurance, guidance, serenity, comfort, and unconditional love, God gave us the Holy Spirit to be with us forever and to reveal his truths and God's will in each of our lives.

Armed with these magnificent truths presented to me by the Holy Spirit, I felt ready to write them down on paper. Usually before writing I try to nourish my body and feed the soul in order to create positive energy around me, but because I had been ill with bronchitis, my cupboards were bare. Each day I put off a trip to the store, hoping I would feel better the next day, but on this day the Holy Spirit nudged me to get up, get dressed, and get to the grocery store. I knew to be obedient when the Spirit whispers. Before getting dressed, I took some time to meditate, and of course, open my mind to the possibilities of a miracle—a daily ritual.

There I was getting my bananas, oranges, multiple bell peppers in an array of colors, broccoli, lettuce, cucumbers, and tomatoes and feeling quite pleased with myself for selecting a wide variety of healthy vegetables. Moving my cart along quite happily, I surveyed the healthy fruit juices. Suddenly, I heard a familiar voice. It was one of the assistant managers whom I occasionally chatted with about Southern cooking and Louisiana gumbo. He was from New Orleans, so our conversation usually was about their delicious foods; however, this time he began the conversation by asking, "How's your book coming along?" It had been months since I'd mentioned my book, *Cuddled in God's Hands*, to him, so I was surprised he was asking about it. But I replied, "Oh, thanks for asking. That book is doing great, but I'm working on a new one about miracles." His eyes lit up and he quickly responded, "Oh, I have so many of those." Surprised because we had never spoken about his spirituality, I told him that I was very glad to hear that he believed in miracles and excited that he was open to the possibilities.

I was about to continue shopping when he stated, "I've got one I can tell you about right now. It happened not too long ago."

He was busy cutting open boxes and taking out sour cream and stacking them. He didn't miss a beat, but I said, "Are you sure you can talk and cut open the boxes at the same time?" He assured me that he'd be fine. Obviously, he was excited about sharing his story.

He had been on his way to pick up his wife, who worked in Sunnyvale. It was about sixty miles away from Tracy. Because of all the evening traffic, he decided to take the back roads, because traffic was never really as bad as the 580 freeway. Without realizing it, he somehow drifted off to sleep. A voice spoke to him, which jolted and startled him. He didn't know where he was at first or where he was headed. He was in a daze, but when he focused his attention, he stared at a huge truck coming head-on straight at him. He was disoriented at first and didn't know why the truck was on his side of the road. Then he realized that it was he who was on the wrong side of the road. He looked to his right to get over and change lanes but there were two cars. He knew he didn't have enough time to speed up and get in front of the car on the right. He looked to the left and there was an embankment, but he had no choice. He decided to chance the embankment. Just when he swerved and was about to put his foot on the brake, he heard a voice that said, "Don't brake." Hearing the voice, he took both feet off the floor and steered with all his might to keep the car steady, but the car was leaning to the side. Suddenly the truck passed and the car to the right sped up and he maneuvered the car back on the road. When he finished his story, smiling, I said, "My goodness, that's the chapter I'm going to write about when I go back home, the Holy Spirit and how he speaks to us." He said, "Well, the Holy Spirit sure was with me. I would not have survived if I had not listened when it told me to take my feet off the brakes. My car probably would have gone over the embankment." We looked at each other and knew instantly that the Holy Spirit had put us together and that this meeting was no chance meeting. I said, "Let me hurry up and finish shopping so I can go home and write your story. You have truly inspired me today." He grinned from ear to ear and with that we did a high-five and I hurried to checkout, ecstatic to get in my car and home to my writing.

Realizing the power of the Holy Spirit within us is unmistakably overwhelming. Moreover, it is important to remember that he is residing in all of us as a counselor, comforter, healer, redeemer, and advisor in times as stress, trials, and tribulations. The Holy Spirit manifests itself sometimes as a sign, a stranger, an unexpected gift, and as I usually exclaim, a guardian angel. The important thing for us to remember is to stop, listen, hear, and act according to his will. As John 14:26 teaches us, "But the Counselor, the Holy Spirit, whom the Father will send in my name, will remind you of everything I have said to you."

God Whispers

God's whisper is calling out to me
My conscience some would say
Telling me what's right and wrong
Thus keeping me safe another day.
Some days I worry much too much
About my life and circumstance
And the troubled world which we live in
This world is full of endless sin.
We need a comforter for us all
Then suddenly God's whisper calls
And calms my inner spirit.
The voice is soothing in my ear
Telling me there's nothing to fear
The Holy Spirit is inside me
Listening quietly is the key.

By Frances Purnell-Dampier

Chapter 4

Steps to Attracting and Recognizing Miracles

Attracting miracles is a unique and intentional skill. Several strategies must occur in order for miracles to be recognizable and consistent in everyday living. The dictionary gives many remarkable definitions of the word *attract*. *Attract* means to evoke, unite, allure, pull, entice, charm, or draw nearby physical force, sensation, or senses. A combination of all or some of these things enables us to experience the awesome power of miracles or blessings from the Holy Spirit. Crediting God for the enchanting masterpiece he has already blessed us with is the first step. Take a look at just one of God's magnificent creatures. Because I have always held a fascination with butterflies as a child,

I marvel at the intricate design of these insects. The monarch butterfly is extremely intriguing. The gigantic wings display orange with black veins running throughout its span. The outer edge of the wing has a thick black velvet border that appears to be perfectly symmetrical. Within the black borders are carefully placed white cylindrical spots arranged in an exact arc around the pattern design of dark and light blocks, whose appearance is that of a precise U, forming the body of the wing. The tip of the wing has bright orange, black, and white colors shaped in a perfect V formation. Looking intently at this magnificent insect assures me that God has powers beyond what a mere mortal can comprehend. Take this one insect and multiply it by the hundreds, thousands, or millions of other insects, animals, flowers, trees, fish, fowl, and human beings on the place called Earth and tell me that our God has not created a magical paradise for us, or as I like to call them, *miracles*.

Remember the book of Genesis 1:1-3, **"In the beginning God created the heavens and the earth. Now the earth was formless and empty, darkness was over the surface of the deep, and the Spirit of God was hovering over the waters."**

Imagine this world empty and void of all the beauty we see in nature today. How sad that would be. Therefore, as a first step to attracting more miracles, we must acknowledge and affirm that

God has already provided us with the miraculous world in which we live. We must view our world through new prisms, realizing God's grace and love for us already.

The next step in our spiritual journey is to begin practicing some easy steps or strategies in our everyday walk with God. In our daily prayers, we must ask God to help us as we strive to implement the strategies outlined in this chapter.

Six Strategies for Attracting Miracles

Step 1: Be open to possibilities

In order to believe and recognize miracles, we need to tap into our sixth sense. We all possess the ability but we close our minds to anything we cannot understand using our five senses. Using the sixth sense enables us to perceive the dimension of the unseen world of angels, ghosts, signs, symbols, and especially perceptions. This ability to activate the sixth sense helps in our spiritual growth. We can develop this spirituality over time by praying for enlightenment and always being present in the moment, expecting the unexpected and being accepting of odd and unusual circumstances.

I tell the story of my mother's death in my book, *Cuddled in God's Hands*. My mother died unexpectedly. She wasn't sick or anything. I went to Mississippi in a daze to bury my mother. I went through the services numb and sad beyond words could express. When I returned to California, I couldn't quite wrap my head around the fact that my mother was no longer around. Several times I picked up the phone to call her when I was cooking to ask her if she put sour cream in the "sock it to me" cake to make it so delicious and moist. But as I dialed the number, I quickly realized that she wasn't going to answer on the other end. My sadness enveloped me in a deep, depressing way.

One night as I lay sleeping, I woke up feeling a presence in the room. I sat up in bed, and to my astonishment there stood my mother at the foot of my bed. At first, she was standing at the right corner of my bed. She was dressed all in white, but it was as if the sparkles emanated from her and her radiance shined all around her. She looked like a beautiful angel. Through telepathy, my mother spoke to me. "Don't worry about me. I am with God. I am in a better place now and in peace. Remember, God needs angels too."

This vision left me shaken and with a greater inner peace, but also a sense of "knowing" that I had experience something supernatural. I had heard my elders speak of ghosts when I was a child as if it was commonplace, but I didn't expect I would ever experience it. This was a miracle of the best kind for me, a visit from my mother. After that, I was open to many possibilities. Anything was possible if you just believed. God's grace gave me the opportunity to see my wonderful mother again, and I was eternally grateful and appreciative to be a child of the most high.

Step 2: Allow yourself to experience a spiritual awakening

Reading spiritual materials and the Holy Bible can help to reveal if you are getting closer to spiritual awakening. It doesn't come overnight. It can take years to tap into this level of consciousness. From my reading, spiritual awakening means to understand your truth. It is an ability to know yourself in a way outside of the normal way people see you. Some authors call it spirit consciousness and being present in all that you do. This is undoubtedly a unique way of attracting a renewal of positive energy. Being spiritual is different from being religious. I was brought up in a religious environment. My stepfather was a Baptist minister. My mother was a member of the women's deacons. We attended church every Sunday not once, but twice. Rising early on Sunday morning, we rushed off to Sunday school. We learned the children's version of biblical stories. Later, we went to regular service and I heard my stepfather give a rousing sermon about Moses, Abraham, King Solomon, or the many miracles of Jesus

Christ. In the evening, we gathered again for what we called night service. The choir sang spirituals until everyone became "happy," which meant people were filled with the Holy Spirit. Church members shouted and cried until an usher came over to fan them to calm them down. In the Baptist church, when the Holy Spirit came upon you, the ushers fanned and fanned. But sometimes we went to the Church of God in Christ. I noticed a difference when church members were overcome with the Holy Spirit. Members shouted, jumped up and down, ran up and down the aisle, and no one touched them. Sometimes they would swirl around and around like a whirlwind, turning and turning. But then something magical would happen to them. They would begin speaking in tongues. I knew something special was going on with these people. They entered another level of consciousness with God. They stepped into an alternative space that went beyond what we know as our reality. They shed the religion and entered into a spiritual realm with God. There in that realm they were able to connect with God on a whole different level. These souls had tapped into an unknown space.

Watching Oprah's "Super Soul Sunday," I was privileged to hear a conversation with Panache Desai. He pretty much summed up what I was attempting to say, **"There's no greater power than to be in harmony with oneself."**

Step 3: Pray and call on God for guidance and assurance

Prayer no doubt changes things in a mighty way. Many studies are being made about the benefits of praying. These studies point out that if you pray a few times a day consistently you can prevent memory loss, Alzheimer's, stress, heart attack, anxiety, and depression, to name a few. Well, that certainly is better than exercising. That fits right into my schedule. God waits for our prayer. He loves it when we connect with him in such a personal way. Some people pray only when they are in trouble, but we must pray in good times and in bad times. Blessings and miracles become abundant and commonplace when we are unselfish and honor God all of the time. For me, miracles are so natural and frequent that throughout my day I thank God and praise his name on a continuous basis.

Worshipping and praying with fellow Christians strengthens your bond and connectedness with God. The more people pray collectively to God, the more explosive the power of the prayer. I have heard of many healings when prayer chains are activated. My mother's sister had two different cancers at the same time. She was given six months to live. Her husband was a minister and asked all the churches to pray collectively for her. After a while she went back to the doctor and they could find no trace of the cancer. That was over twenty-five years ago and she is still living and praising God. In Matthew 18:20, Jesus said, "For where two or three come together in my name, then I am in the midst of them."

Step 4: Draw positive energy into your life

In order to attract positives, you must weed out the negatives. Negative people and thoughts deplete your energy. Negativity causes self-doubt, unhappiness, and can crush your joy and inner wellbeing. People who think positively do not let negative things get them down. They expect good things to happen to them and good things do occur because they almost will them into being. To attract miracles and positive energy, you must have an optimistic view of the world around you. Sometimes it is difficult to be cheerful and optimistic. This is when you must push through your misery and pull that renewal energy back to the surface. I remember when I was a teacher, being a wife and mother of three boys sometimes would drain me of my energy over the weekend, especially if the family spent the weekend on a family outing, as was usually the case.

Being drained of most of my energy, I knew I had to be alert and ready for action on Monday morning. Middle school students going through puberty expected fun and exciting, motivating lessons. In an attempt to regain much needed energy, I would do two things. First, I had this incredible beautiful red dress that was very flattering. Whenever I wore it, I got tons of compliments from the staff, which helped lift my spirits before I even got to my first period class, so I went into my closet and pulled out the red dress. Next, I pulled out my no-fail lesson plan: a popcorn treat for students. If all students turned in homework the week before, they were promised a popcorn party. I began the day with sustained silent reading from their novels. While they read, I quietly went to the back of the room, turned on the popcorn machine, and filled thirty-two bags of popcorn to the brim. While they quietly read, I stopped by each desk and handed them a popcorn snack to actually eat while they read. Their eyes looked at me with adoration and gratitude. That started each period on a positive note and the rest of the period went absolutely wonderful. The students were so happy and content that by the end of the day, I felt invigorated myself and ready for the rest of the week.

Step 5: Expect a miracle to happen in all circumstances

> **"Jesus loves me**
>
> **This I know**
>
> **For the Bible**
>
> **Tells me so"**

Singing this song during Sunday-school class for children cemented early in my young mind that Jesus loved me and would take care of me no matter what. There was never a doubt that when trouble came my way God would watch over me. My mother, a deaconess, and my stepfather, a minister, never let me forget that God had protected me by pouring out his "blessing" on me. My stepfather often preached about God's magnificent grace. He would have the congregation recite "I am a child of God" several times in unison. Surely, he would say, "If you are a child of the most high, he would never forsake you in your times of need."

Because of these early teachings, I was certain that God favored me and would take care of me always. As I became older and more understanding of my relationship with God in a deeper, more spiritual way, the word "blessing" evolved into the word *miracle*. To me, the words are synonymous and more in tune with modern-day thinking and philosophies. Whatever term you use, it is clear that God, Jesus, or the Holy Spirit is omnipotent and intervenes on our behalf each day. When the intervention occurs, a miracle or blessing has certainly occurred!

Second nature to me is recognizing all the miracles that envelop my life. Take for example my first ever trip to New York. After retirement, I developed a bucket list of places I wanted to travel to. As luck would have it—or as some would say, unluckily—the first available timeslot for my timeshare was in March. The only timeshare close to New York was located in Atlantic City, New Jersey. That was a lucky break for me, or should I say, miracle, because I loved playing the slots. I invited my best friend and younger sister to come along. They were excited about the trip, but they both chided me, saying the weather was going to be freezing. For some reason, the Holy Spirit kept telling me not to worry about the weather conditions, so I quickly retorted back to them that the weather was going to be fine. Of course, they did not believe me because they had both been to New York before and I had not. For me, I was stepping out on faith alone.

When we arrived in Atlantic City, it was a little chilly. We went shopping to get hats and scarves. There were blocks of high-end stores and fabulous bargains to boot. When a cold breeze crossed our paths, my sister and girlfriend looked at me with the "I told you so" affirmations. The timeshare was absolutely gorgeous, overlooking the New Jersey boardwalk. Looking back now, a year later, I consider it a miracle that we were able to see that beautiful landscape before the disastrous hurricane Sandy totaled it.

We became quite adventurous and decided to take a Greyhound bus to New York, something we hadn't done since our college days. Making it safely to the Big Apple was a real treat. Walking off the bus was an incredible surprise. The weather was spectacular. In fact, it was seventy-three degrees and my sister and friend looked at me in amazement. Of course, I said, "Miracle!" Arriving at the New Yorker Hotel was another miracle, because it was within walking distance of all the marvelous sights.

The day after we arrived, we decided to look for this well-known restaurant where they make breakfast items sculpted like exotic flowers. Striking out walking with a map at our side, we walked and walked. When we arrived near the address of the restaurant, we surveyed the buildings but could not spot the restaurant's sign. We walked up and down the street, and when we were totally disappointed, my best friend's daughter, who had joined us, decided to look up the restaurant on her BlackBerry. To our amazement, she shouted, "It's inside a hotel. Let's look for the hotel!" Suddenly we turned around, and to our amazement, the restaurant was right in front of us. Again, I shouted, "It's a miracle."

After breakfast, our adventure continued. We wanted to find the double-decker buses that we heard were the best way to see the whole city. The map suggested that the bus depot was only a few blocks away from the restaurant. We found the street, and as we looked for the sign, we spotted a double-decker bus parked at the corner. My friend ran ahead of us, excited to see the bus driver standing outside the bus. She engaged in a conversation with him, and by the time we caught up with her, she beckoned us to go with her to the souvenir shop across the street from the bus. Puzzled, we went with her, but as soon as we got there, we asked her why we were there. She said the bus driver told her that the usual price was $44.00 per person, but because we looked like his cousins and such nice ladies, we could go free. Unbelievable, but we weren't questioning God's miracles, so we jumped aboard. The sights were spectacular and breathtaking. We traveled all over the city, taking in Times Square, Madison Square Garden, the Statue of Liberty, Central Park, and the Empire State Building, to name a few. We sat on the top level, so we got to take in the fabulous view. Feeling guilty for such an incredible tour, we all decided to tip him twenty dollars each. He was totally shocked when we exited and handed him the money.

Continuing our adventure that night was going to be enjoyable because we were eating at the soul food restaurant, B. Smiths, and afterward attending the off-Broadway play *Sistas*. The hotel staff directed us to the restaurant, which again required no cab, easy walking distance. We thought we might need a cab to take us to the play, so we left a little time in between to make sure we would get there in plenty of time. The food at B. Smith's was divine! The greens with smoked turkey, sweet potatoes, and fried chicken for me took me back to my Mississippi childhood memories. After slurping every morsel of food from our plates, we decided to set out to find the play. We asked the waiter if he knew where St. Luke's Theater was and to our amazement he pointed to two doors down the street. What do you think we all said at the same time? You got it, "Miracle!" By this time, my sister and friend had become true believers or converts of the power of miracles. When we arrived home, we told everyone about all the miracles that occurred during our trip. Spreading the word about God's miracles helps God's message to travel and be heard by more and more believers.

Step 6: Make time to meditate daily to attract all that is good and holy

Meditation is a natural way to get in touch with your inner spirit. Taking a little time each day to meditate is important even if it's five or ten minutes a day. Meditating helps to focus and concentrate, enabling us to make more intelligent decisions. It helps to ground or center our thoughts on the Holy Spirit and clears the mind of mundane daily activities.

For three years, I spent three days a week taking yoga classes at my local gym. Yoga is a great way to connect the mind, body, and spirit. It has a way of clearing the mind and balancing the body. Yoga is intended to provide inner calmness and serenity. Oftentimes, I would stop by the gym after work to relieve the inner stresses of the workday. The yoga techniques of proper breathing through meditation and posture exercises helped release anxiety and tension in the body. We did different stretches, poses, and counting as we held stances for a certain number of seconds.

These stretches helped me to learn control of breathing, which in real life came in handy when situations occurred at work. Instead of reacting right away to a crisis, I learned to breathe first more slowly to decrease my heart rate, thereby enabling me to make a more decisive, well-thought-out proactive response. Yoga, I found, is a great prescription for being balanced physically, mentally, emotionally, and spiritually. Yoga is only one way to achieve this meditative process. It is important for each person to find their own avenue to successful meditation. The most important factor in all of this is to find more ways to tune in to the Spirit within each of us.

Chapter 5

Miraculous Stories by Everyday People

These miracle stories are from friends and fellow Christians who honored God by testifying to the true miracles of his amazing grace in their lives. The stories are breathtaking, courageous, inspirational, shockingly honest, and utterly engaging as they recap events in their lives that without the presence of the Holy Spirit could have tumbled them into a world of utter despair in many cases. By their courage in telling these stories, others will gain confidence, knowing that their particular circumstance can also turn into a positive if they just believe and trust in the power of God's goodness. Once you put your life in God's hands and turn your troubles over to him, you will develop a relationship like no other and your life will never be the same. The miracles that occurred in the lives of the writers will live on to inspire and enrich the lives of many others. The book of Matthew 28:19 says, **"Therefore go and make disciples of all nations . . ."**

Eleven Miracle Stories

Cancer Miracle

by D.G, Bay Area

I was born in Canada in 1958, the eldest of four siblings. I moved to a small island in western New York when I was five. It was a small town, predominantly white upper-class, where everyone knew everyone else's business, except ours. All anyone saw on the outside was the quaint little white house with a family of four very well-behaved children. Little did they know what was going on in the little house on a daily basis.

I was sexually, physically, and emotionally abused from nine years old onward by my father. I ran away at sixteen but could not make it on my own. My nickname was "Ugly." I witnessed horrible things in that little house on the island that no child should ever have to see or go through. When it was brought to my mother's attention, she at first didn't believe me/us (denial), and then many years later when she finally let it sink in what my dad had done, she took his side and never left him. I wanted nothing more to do with my family ever again.

-I drank at a very young age

-I was married, had two boys, and divorced by twenty-one

-I lost custody of my youngest son

-I got involved with a married man, lived with him for over twelve years; he became abusive

-I was in a deadly car crash and survived

-I went through a horrible breakup where he tried to kill me

-I left on a train in the middle of the night with my three-year-old to escape

-I was on the run and always looking over my should from his threats for years

-I was given full custody of my daughter

-I have no relationship with my youngest son

-I had fallen and injured my back, healing with no surgery

-My eldest son was killed in a murder/suicide

-My daughter was in a deadly car crash and survived

-I had stage four cervical cancer and survived

Throughout my life God had always been with me. When I was nine years old and in third grade, my teacher asked me one day if I would like to go to Sunday school with her (she was the Sunday school teacher too) and her daughter, who was my age. And I went with her. I found God, or should I say, God found me, his lost sheep. I have heard God's voice call me "My child." I have felt his hands on my face, and when I needed it the most, I have felt him hold me up because I just couldn't stand on my own anymore. I don't know why these things happened to me, but I do know that they have made me a better person, a stronger woman, and with each experience I have become closer to God. And through everything I have been through, I have never had any therapy—God is my therapist!

When the doctors told me I had the "big C," I said, "What?" "You have stage three cervical cancer and it is inoperable." I had a tumor the size of a large baseball but the cancer had also spread to many other organs as well. At first I couldn't really comprehend what they were telling me but from the day I started hemorrhaging (where doctors said they would do everything possible) through all the chemotherapy and external radiation, I found hope and calm through prayer and through my daughter's prayers for me. I tried to always think positively even though it was very difficult. God was always by my side!

Prior to the doctors starting my first round of chemo, there was a month where they were waiting for approval from my insurance carrier to give me the procedure. In that timeframe my tumor had doubled and was now the size of a large grapefruit and very painful. The cancer had now begun to affect my kidneys and they began shutting down. The cancer had now become a stage four. Doctors had to rush me into the operating room; it was at that time my daughter was told that they will do everything that they could for me. When I was able to go home, my daughter said to me that she was scared because if something had happened to me she had no family. Just because I didn't have or want a relationship with them doesn't mean that she didn't want one. I thought about it. I wasn't scared to die. I needed to make sure that everything was in order for her in case I did die, and one of the things I needed to do was to contact my family, for her and for me. My daughter now has family and I am in contact with everyone except my dad and my son. But give it time; God works miracles in my life all the time!

The first round of chemo and radiation didn't work, so the doctors had to wait another month to try an internal radiation procedure from Europe called Brachytherapy. After this procedure I had to wait another six weeks before I could be examined to see if it shrank the tumor. The waiting was the hardest part, even over the procedures. We/I did a lot of praying. After the exam, the tumor had shrunk and the procedure worked! I now am cancer free. Doctors say that it is highly likely that the cancer will come back within a year, but I have faith that it won't! I have one more reconstructive surgery to go through and then I should be back to my old self again. It has been a very long journey but one I could not have gone through without God or my friends and family. Don't ever give up! Just look up and ask the almighty God for help; he always hears us!

Believe me, going through cancer was one of the hardest things I have ever had to endure, but a positive came from a negative: I have my family back. In my heart of hearts I knew that I should forgive and I now have but I will *never* forget, and it affects me every day of my life. And because of what I have experienced, I can honestly tell someone that I *know* how they feel. You can only say that when you have gone through what they have gone through and understand their pain or grief. Without God's help and his army of angels I would not and could not have survived the life I was dealt. I may never know why my life was/is the way it was/is, but God has plans for me! Big plans!

Anything
and Everything

by J. L., East Bay

"He can fix anything (and everything) . . ." The lyrics swirled in my mind as I drove to my appointment at the diagnostic imaging department of my local hospital. An ultrasound examination had been ordered by my personal physician, as it would help in identifying the nature of a dark mass that had shown up in my right breast on two successive mammograms taken the previous month.

While doing some Internet research on breast ultra sonograms, I found out that a large percentage of women who are referred for this type of exam show some kind of malignancy. I knew that I needed to be prepared emotionally, and most importantly spiritually, for whatever the Lord had allowed to develop in my body.

As I went through the days of waiting for my exam, I shared this burden with my friend Frances Dampier, the dynamic site administrator of the elementary school in the South San Francisco Bay Area district where I taught fifth grade. I knew Frances to be a wise, godly, and compassionate leader, and I was confident that she was a person I could trust to uphold me, not only in prayer, but with good advice as well.

The following day, Frances handed me a CD by a singer whose talents and inspiration I learned to appreciate greatly. The album was called *Food for the Spirit*. The singer was Smokey Robinson. Frances asked me to take the CD home and listen to it. She smiled and assured me that the songs would help strengthen my faith. I discovered that she was right. The songs "Standing on Jesus" and "I Praise and Worship You, Father" were a great encouragement to me. However, the one song that truly stuck in my soul and caused me to sing along with increasing enthusiasm was called "He Can Fix Anything (and Everything)." These words buoyed me up each time I was tempted to sink into doubt and fear as the day of the exam loomed ever closer.

The nurse who performed the ultrasound examination was quiet and friendly. She began moving the ultrasound sensor over the area where the X-ray pictures showed the dark spot. The screens were all behind me and out of my sight. I looked only at the ceiling and implored the Lord to be in complete control of all that this exam would reveal. As the test progressed, I could hear the clicking sounds as the nurse took still pictures of what she could see. She then began to move the sensor over a wider area. Sensing that this could possibly mean a bigger problem than just a single mass, I begged the Lord for strength to deal with whatever he might be allowing to happen. The nurse informed me that she needed to go and consult the radiologist for evaluation of the images she had taken. After ten minutes she returned and began again to move the sensor over my right breast, repeating the process of the first time around. Aware that this extended exam could very well mean a huge change in my whole life, I surrendered to the presence of God and to all he would carry me through in the coming weeks, months, or even years.

After what seemed like an eternity, the nurse announced that we were finished and that I could go. She informed me that my gynecologist would call me to let me know the results of my ultrasound. Two days later, I returned home from school late in the afternoon to find a message alert blinking on my telephone. Dr. Andrea's friendly voice came on to tell me she had "good news" to share with me. She said, "Judy, the radiologists who evaluated your ultrasound images report that they could not find any sign of the spot that was on your mammograms. I am so happy to be able to report this to you." I stood transfixed in front of my telephone, repeatedly pressing the "play" button to listen again and again to this astounding news. I became aware that my savior and friend Jesus Christ was an invisible companion in the room, that he shared my joy and enjoyed my relief, a gift from his own hand!

I looked up and sang a song to him: "He Can Fix Anything (and Everything)."

Miracles

by M. P., East Bay

These three stories happened to me several years ago. This was during a period of time in my life where I was searching for God with my whole being, heart, soul, and body. I was praying many hours a day, seeking the Lord in prayer, praying to the Holy Spirit, Bible study, starting a Bible club for the students of Bishop School, and attending many church gatherings of believers. During my daily tasks during this time of my life, I was in deep intercession for strangers standing in lines, walking down sidewalks, and prayed almost constantly in my daily activities. This period of my life was an intense God period, unlike any other in my walk except for the first "honeymoon" period when I had just heard the Good News and had accepted Christ as my savior while in college many years prior.

I cannot really explain why this period of time occurred in my life, as my life has now returned to a much more normal pace. All I know is that I saw miracles happen to people I knew and to myself during this time. The three that I care to share are just the most dramatic and most notable, but this is not meant to negate the other God moments I had during this period of time.

Miracle no. 1: The wedding ring

This happened on Easter morning several years ago. I woke up early, like I do often, and had a deep desire to spend some quiet time with Jesus before church. I went on about a 2½ mile walk in my neighborhood, where I have been known to walk a common established route. And throughout the walk I was praying and singing and listening to gospel music, and completely happy, knowing I was close to God. I came home and got ready for church the normal way and did not notice until my hands were raised over my head in the middle of the church service that the 1.2-carat diamond in my wedding ring had disappeared! I was rather shocked, but just continued through the church service without saying anything except to my husband. I just prayed that God would help me find it! I told my friends at church to look on the carpet and let me know if they found anything.

After I got home, I was bummed; therefore, I decided to retrace my steps all the way back through the miles that I had walked, praying and walking while searching, to no avail. I went on with the Easter day as normal with my family, cooking and washing dishes and every so often looking all over the carpet floors of my house, hoping by some chance the diamond would appear. When I went to bed that night, just before I went to sleep I confessed to God that this diamond ring being lost was ruining my peace and destroying my fellowship with him, and I confessed that it was taking up way too much of my attention. And then I just gave it to him to deal with. I was done. After all, it was just a ring, it was not as important as my dear husband, and certainly not worth getting all upset about. I said I could be happy with a fake cubic zirconium if need be, and went to sleep to forget about it.

The next morning was a school day, and as usual I needed to race to get ready and out the door on time. I said hi to the Lord as I woke up, and as soon as I realized I was awake, I felt a huge desire to go check the carpet right by my dresser. It was as if I woke up and was driven by a motor to go check this one part of my room. The diamond was right on the carpet, where I always got dressed. I yelled to my husband, "I found it!" Neither he nor I have ever been able to figure why we never saw it there before.

I have always wondered if an angel returned it in the middle of the night.

Miracle no. 2: The coffee cup

This happened in my classroom in Room 14 at Bishop Elementary School. It happened right after, maybe a few months after, the diamond-reappearing miracle. It was morning, maybe 9:00 AM.

It was just a few days after a major vacation break, and I was really sleepy and feeling unenergetic that day. It was on a Monday, because I had Bible club that afternoon and I would be the teacher. I needed all the pep I could get!

I decided to make myself a cup of instant coffee, so I put the hot water heater on, which was in a corner of classroom, and went back to teaching. When the water came to a boil, I picked up my coffee cup and realized it was not completely clean. So I poured some of the boiling hot water in it, all the way to the top, and some liquid soap so that it would get sparkly clean. Just then, one of my students came up and asked me a quick question, and because I was in a hurry to get back to teaching, I mistakenly put my hand into the cup to wash it out. I had my hand in boiling hot water! Many years ago, I had a finger accident and I have to wear my wedding ring on my right hand. So my right hand was completely hot, and I put it immediately in cold water at the sink. I immediately realized the danger I had created for myself, and under my breath I said a quick prayer, "Please, Jesus, help me! Don't let this be a bad burn!"

After I said that prayer, I immediately went back to teaching without even thinking about my hand. My students needed me and my attention and I was no longer sleepy! I never did drink that cup of coffee!

I taught the rest of the day and all through Bible club, and went home normally that night like nothing out of the usual had happened that day! I literally forgot about it. It was completely erased from my mind! I did not even tell my husband. It was as if it had never happened. My hand was completely normal; there was absolutely no sign whatsoever of any burn.

The next morning, as usual, I got up early to go swimming before school, and I always take off my wedding ring and set it on top of the microwave until I got home. I just don't like to swim with it on in case something might happen to it in the pool.

My husband greeted me at the door after I came home from my swim, as he had noticed that my ring looked weird. He asked me, "What the heck did you do yesterday that would cause your ring to look like this?"

I was embarrassed to tell him, but did tell him what happened the day before. Both he and I were aware at that moment that a miracle had occurred. My ring was completely out of shape; it was no longer round. It had molded itself to the shape of my finger, and it was completely distorted and bent out of shape. It looked as if someone had taken the metal and just banged it hard to reshape it to a weird, distorted shape. It was completely deformed, but still intact. The diamond itself was the same.

I took the ring to my favorite jeweler, the one who had heard the ring miracle no. 1 and fixed it that time.

Now I was back with another miracle story. When I told him, he said that the gold had melted to the shape of my finger and that could only happened at extremely high temperatures, and that I should have been in the emergency room immediately after that happened. He testified that another miracle had happened to my ring; that could be the only explanation in his professional experience.

Praise God! I should have been disfigured, but instead he supernaturally intervened and healed my hand!

Miracle no. 3: The jewelry box

This was a dream. I dreamed that I was in a glorious room that was filled from floor to ceiling with extravagantly decorated jewelry boxes. The entire room was so brilliant that your eyes could barely stand the reflection of the light. The boxes ranged in sizes, but all were completely covered in radiant diamonds. I felt as if I was in the jewelry storeroom of heaven.

I bent down to see one of the jewelry boxes and I realized that the boxes had tickets on them. One part of the ticket said "Admit One" and the other part had a name on it. I asked what the names meant, and the Lord told me that these were his children, his jewels.

I woke up realizing that some of those names were the names of students I had once taught!

The Lord, I feel, was telling me how happy he was with the Bishop Bible Club!

By Mary Pound

My Baby Brother

by D. M., Northern California

My dear little brother was a very strong person who adored God. He used to always tell me that he wanted to be a priest and I told him that he had to grow up first and learn a little about life, and maybe he would have some other interests. Johnny was six and I was about sixteen years older and was into boxing. He used to put the gloves on and work out with me and he would start to come and throw punches every which way and I used to correct him, "Little brother, you have to learn to keep the punches above the beltline." He was the "Johnny come lately baby," as my mother was in her forties. We had a dear friend named Kieran who was a Christian brother at St. Boniface Church. Johnny became ill with what we thought was the flu but he was finally admitted to the hospital for a checkup. He was diagnosed with leukemia. Finally, after being there for a time, it was determined that his condition was incurable. He was so religious that he made whichever nun or nurse was caring for him take him to the chapel every day and placed a crucifix across his shoulder. When Johnny was finally back home, our friend Kieran visited him, and Johnny told us that he wanted to speak to Kieran alone. As I can remember, Kieran was with Johnny for about a half-hour. When Kieran came back from visiting Johnny, he told us that Johnny told him that he would be with God within one week, which was a holy holiday, All Saints' Day, November 1. Johnny passed away on that day.

My Miracle Baby

by S. P., Northern California

My husband and I dreamed of having a beautiful baby girl and fortunately we found out that I was indeed expecting a girl. We went to the doctor and even heard the song "Isn't She lovely" by Stevie Wonder and were convinced this was a sign from God. Needless to say, we were ecstatic.

At twenty-four weeks' gestation, I began feeling some pains. I was leading a school through its accreditation process and was in the middle of the meeting when all of a sudden I began profusely bleeding. I began shaking, went downstairs, and the school secretary rushed me to the hospital. When I was checked, the doctor told me that I was losing the baby and placed a pan under me "just in case." I was devastated. My husband rushed to the hospital and we were utterly heartbroken as doctors came in and said that we would have to sign papers to keep the baby alive even if she were to have severe deformities, neurological damage, and other defects. We obviously signed, and just prayed and prayed. They kept taking us to the sonography room, and at that time, a nurse whispered to me that I would be okay and held my hand, saying she was a lay-sister of Mother Theresa's order and that she was praying, that I would be well, and with a healthy baby. I held her hand and was scared out of my mind. The only person to comfort me was that unnamed, unknown, mysterious nurse

The next day, my father visited me at the hospital because my husband was at work. He sat in my hospital room as I lay in bed and began talking about his mother, my paternal grandmother who was a survivor of the Armenian genocide and happened to be a nurse/midwife. I have always considered her an inspiration, one who has survived in the face of adversity, and we began to talk about "what she would have said" and "how she would have lightened up the mood" if she saw what was happening. Right when we were having that discussion, a nurse knocked on my door and said, "Hello, I want to talk to you as a friend of the Armenians." We were shocked and welcomed her, asking her how she knew I was Armenian, and it was through seeing my last name, which like all Armenians', ends in—*ian*. She then closed the door and said, "I am a midwife, and I want to tell you how to get through this and get better. You are to eat dried apricots, which are hematocrit makers, and visualize positive things happening to your body. Rest assured, you are going to be fine, and your daughter will be safe and you will not go into labor this early." My father and I were shocked. We felt my grandmother's presence; God's presence was there and he sent these angels to protect me and my family. The next day, another doctor came in and told me that I was okay, that my situation had stabilized, and although I was better, I was to stay in bed rest for the remainder of my pregnancy. My daughter was born at almost thirty-five weeks, almost ten weeks later. And although she was premature, she was perfect and healthy, and to this day remains a positive, healthy, miracle child. We named her "Areni," which in Armenian means "gift from heaven." She is indeed a gift from God, as all babies are. And ten years later, we are enjoying all of her miracles.

Every day I thank God for his angels, who guide me through every trial and tribulation. Whether it is for my daughter's continued health or the little miracles he places in my path, or for the guidance of the angels that are always around me.

In Loving Memory of My Son

by S. S., Northern California

Psalm 34:18

The Lord is close to the brokenhearted and saves those who are crushed in spirit.

And thus the story of simply one of my many miraculous gifts from my Lord, the Almighty.

The horrible phone call that changed my life forever arrived in the wee hours of the morning on December 9, 2002. Slumber had always come easily for me, a time to rest my soul and quiet the mind. I was deeply sound asleep. The words resonated like a lingering knife piercing my heart: a horrible accident . . . severely injured by a drunk driver. What came out of my mouth was foreign; the wail was long and animalistic. Within twelve hours, my only child, Jason, was pronounced brain dead at the age of twenty-seven. His partner, Kristin, was one-month pregnant. My heart was shredded, broken, collapsed, and weeping. My soul was covered in desolation. I was left with the "essence" of my son, a broken person.

The birth of my granddaughter was incontestably bittersweet; however, I fell in love immediately. She was born on a sunny and warm August day, with a noticeable gentle breeze. The perfect setting for a new birth. Alexandra Jace's baptism was set for two months later in a Catholic church in Indiana (where Kristin had gone to be with her parents). The trip for the baptism was marked by sadness, as seemingly the whole year was. My husband, who was chosen to be the godfather, could not attend due to mitigating circumstances at work. I, the chosen godmother, was solo in my flight and seemingly in my thoughts. I brought Jason's baptismal candle, several framed photos of him and my broken heart. He would witness the baptism, if only in pictures. I so wanted him there. Arriving in Indiana the night before gave Kristin, her mother, and I time to grieve together. Kristin's parents had divorced, so the sacred event was to be witnessed by only us three women and one two-month-old child. This seemed to add to the disparity of the event and clouded with shrouds what should have been a joyous occasion—to witness a child blessed into the life of Christianity. Tears were readily falling on our way to St. Joseph's Church that Sunday morning and we couldn't stop. The mass was further interrupted with the sound of shrill cries coming from baby Alexandra. Kristin forgot the bottle and Alexandra's perception of "quiet" at mass was not yet instilled. After mass, Fr. Bernie solemnly walked toward us and informed us he needed to have a private conversation. Apparently, there were two families baptizing children that day. One that had ceremoniously brought their extended families and had a gathering of over thirty people, and us. Would we mind if he were to baptize Alexandra first, as the second baptism would most likely be lengthy? With Alexandra's stomach still churning for food, we gladly agreed. I walked to the altar, placed Jason's beautifully framed picture, lit his baptismal candle, and cried. The tears were coming so fast I didn't bother to wipe them away. At that point, Fr. Bernie asked, albeit politely, where the godfather was? We explained to him that my husband was not able to attend, as much as he wanted to be there. Of course this brought more weeping and sadness. Fr. Bernie continued to explain that we would need a male figure to witness the baptism in my husband's place, and that my husband would still be listed as the godfather. We froze. Neither Kristin nor her mother knew anyone else in the small town, much less a male. Once again I began to cry, holding the picture of Jason tightly against my heart and wondering if life could possibly get worse. At that moment Fr. Bernie asked if it would be okay if he asked someone from the other baptismal group if they were willing to stand in as a witness. Moments later he returned with a handsome young man who looked to be in his mid-twenties. The entire experience thus far seemed surreal, which seemed to mimic my pervasive existence. At the moment the young man walked over all I could think was why can't my son be here? I extended my hand to shake the young man's extended hand as he said, "Hello, my name is Jason." I looked at Kristin, whose knees were buckling, grabbed her arm to steady her, felt a peaceful, warm glow take over my entire body, and knew without a doubt that I had just experienced a miracle. The miraculous, infinite glory of God!

—Sandra Pertile Summers, in honor of my son,

Jason Christopher Pertile

Praying in Tongues

by C. G., San Joaquin Valley

The first time I heard someone speak in tongues, it was in church. It was right after the choir sang. I was surprised but not too surprised, because I remembered it had been written in the Bible.

The second time I heard it was at a retreat, and this time when the interpretation was given I felt a zing of electricity go through my body and I was overcome with emotion.

Shortly after, I joined the intercessory prayer group from our church. I heard the other people praying in tongues. So during prayer I asked someone to pray for me to receive the gift of praying in tongues. But it didn't manifest right away. A few months later a lady from the prayer team said that I should just pray what I think I hear the spirit saying. I wasn't sure what I was hearing, so nothing happened.

Then one day, when I was at home, I told myself that I was just going to pray what I thought I heard. As soon as I said it, I immediately was praying in tongues.

I was so surprised. I prayed in tongues for like an hour because I didn't know if I should stop! My husband and kids witnessed it and didn't want to disturb me, so they left to get something to eat.

Finally, I figured I could stop, and I remember thinking, "Wow! I had no idea how real God was until this happened." It was an absolute miracle!

Now I pray in tongues often. I pray in tongues especially when I don't know what to pray because the Bible says the Holy Spirit knows how to pray. I also pray when I sense the Holy Spirit wanting me to pray, and that can happen anywhere and anytime. Sometimes I pray in my sleep and I wake up and continue praying until I feel that I can stop. And it comforts me, because I know that the Holy Spirit is interceding on my or someone I know's behalf.

It is really a gift and I am so very thankful for it!

Praise God!

Hawaii's Road
to Hana

by C. D., East Bay

Every summer my wife and I plan a family trip together with my two daughters. This year was no exception, and we were all especially excited because we were going to beautiful Maui, Hawaii. As usual, I had mapped out some fun and intriguing tours for our days there.

On this particular day, we were going to visit the famous Road to Hana. Maui wouldn't be complete without a tour to this magnificent place, we were told. The Road to Hana was an all-day trip filled with God's handiwork. Some say the sights were as close to Heaven as one could get. The towering waterfalls were majestic and stunning, and the lush green landscape was spectacular. Clear, sparkling beaches surrounded curving mountainsides. This truly was amazing.

So there we were, driving along the beautiful landscape in our rented convertible Mustang without a care in the world. It started sprinkling a little on the way as is known to happen in that part of the country, so I put the top up for a while. The roads were winding with blind turns, high cliffs, and one-lane roads over bridges, but we didn't care because we were having a great time. The girls were sitting in the back, chatting back and forth with me and their mom about the lovely sights. The sun was still gleaming down upon us and pretty soon the girls started asking if I could let the top back down because the rain had stopped. I let it down to get some fresh air in for a while. We all got out a couple of times to view some sacred sights and other scenery. After visiting and taking a dip in the pools of Ohe'o (a.k.a. Seven Sacred Pools), we decided it was getting late and started to make our way back to the resort. As we were headed back, something kept telling me to put the top up. I thought it was rather odd because it wasn't raining. However, the voice in my head was persistent. As I began to put the top up, the girls were yelling for me to keep it down, but I persisted on rolling up the top. Halfway back to the resort, with the girls sulking in the backseat, we heard a large thud on the top of the car, right above where the girls were seated. The girls were frightened as the loud sound startled all of us. We all looked around, wondering what in the heck had landed on the top of the car, but it was too difficult to pull over on the winding road. Hastily, we headed back to the hotel and got out to inspect the car. To our surprise, there was a big dent exactly where one of my daughters was sitting. One of the Hawaiians said it was probably a coconut because it was more common than people think that some people who sit under coconut trees die of head injuries from falling coconuts. Wow! We all thought how lucky we were. As years passed and I became more in tune with God's grace and miracles, I realized that God's voice was what I had heard telling me to close the top on the car. Now, when I hear that voice in my head, I listen. God doesn't steer us wrong.

Barren to Bounty

by S. C., East Bay

When I was a growing up, it was in a house of anger and pain because of alcohol. I had a mother who loved me dearly and was a peaceful, gentle soul, sorely equipped to handle the brutality of a demon-driven drunk whom she loved unequivocally. She knew who he was down inside.

I, on the other hand, did not have the knowledge of who my father was before he fell to drink. I didn't remember his laughter or his kindness. I didn't know what a wonderful person he was inside. I grew up with a person who was tormented by his own childhood and caught in the alcoholism that was prevalent through every line of his family.

My father was a rising star in his world of satellite design, holding scads of patents, the darling of his company, and working on multimillion and several billion-dollar satellite projects. And he was a drunk. The more he drank, the meaner he got. The meaner he got, the more disgusted he was with himself, the more he drank. He was the snake eating his tail and poisoning himself.

I had two younger brothers. Randy, four years my younger, was born with ADHD and severe dyslexia. I truly didn't understand a word he said until he was about six years old. He bounced off the walls and was a human dynamo out of control and needed oh so much help as a kid. Jimmy, a year younger than Randy, was a moody, sensitive, reactive kid. He's the one my dad focused his anger on the most. The one who reminded my dad of himself; he's the one who got lost. At the height of my dad's alcoholic years when I was a teenager, Mom was gone to a PTA meeting or a CHAC or a CANHC meeting or any other meeting that granted her escape and a way to feel like a contributing member of society. When my dad was the worst, I would hide in my closet with a flashlight under the covers, trying to drown out the ugliness and the fighting.

We were the broken family. All of us were good people, all of us trapped, all of us reactionary. And all of this painted my spirit in desperation and feelings of worthlessness. I could see what a family was supposed to be. I knew most people did not grow up the way I did. I knew that I must not be worth anything, because no one cherished me the way I saw other kids were cherished. And I knew that God might love everyone else, but I couldn't earn it, and I wasn't one of the precious ones. I went to church with my neighbor, learned my lessons, and never believed that God actually loved me, because he couldn't. I didn't have a bright soul, I didn't think pure thoughts all the time. I didn't follow all the rules. I was the one that wasn't supposed to be created and the one he'd made a mistake on. My dad used to tell me to stop breathing. I made too much noise, just stop breathing. No one worth loving would be told that by their father. God couldn't love a creature who wasn't even supposed to breathe.

My childhood was a raw sore, peppered with emotional abuse at home and being beaten up, bullied, and ridiculed at school. I was devastatingly alone and my self-deprecating feelings colored everything I did as a kid. I was not a likable kid, but I never did anything wrong on purpose. There was never the thought, "Oh, let's see what I can throw a monkey wrench into today." I tried to be invisible

My next-door neighbors were solid churchgoers. We never went to church in my family; at least, almost never. I don't remember going with my family ever when I was young. I was taught about right and wrong, taught to talk to the Lord, taught to trust him. My parents were raised in the church and my father considered being a preacher when he was in college. So although we weren't a religious home, the influence was always there. I wasn't taught to believe that I would be loved by God though.

Stacy asked me to start coming to church with them. When I approached my mom about going with Stacy, she let me go but never went with me to see what the church was about. I dove into the society of the church, and two years later started going to catechism, learning about being a good Episcopalian. It was so foreign to me in so many ways. To be confirmed, I had to be baptized. I was baptized an hour before I was confirmed. My mother didn't know about the church. And when I was confirmed, where all the other girls were in virginal white, I was in a red dress. I was laughed at and I was gawked at. I had worn red.

Performing that social *faux pas* embarrassed me so much I pulled away from the church. I don't know if I was judged for that or not, but I *knew* what a mistake I'd made and couldn't go back. I was mortified. I had painted myself scarlet. I had shown the church that I wasn't worthy of attending with them. My days of the church were over and the red signified the new trend in my life. I avoided home. I stayed out late. I didn't pay attention to my classes. Where I was attached somewhat to a traditional life before the confirmation, afterward I completely turned away from the church—not my beliefs, but organized religion.

Through this painful growing up, I learned to channel my feelings—my hurt, my love, my loneliness, my insecurities, my anger—into my art. I learned I could escape in my pictures, but I never in a million years would have believed then that I'd end up as a professional artist.

So now, let's fast forward. I married a sailor when I was just nineteen to get out of my parents' house and it was such a bad decision. He was a very nice guy, a great friend but lousy husband material. He was supposed to be my savior, my knight in shining armor, my solution. How dare he not be able to be Superman!

Ricky was transferred from Mountain View, California to Meridian, Mississippi. Ricky was in hog heaven. He was an addicted fisherman and hunter and had no interest in doing anything "cityish." I was alone all the time. I couldn't find a job. I stopped looking. Ricky was gone *all* the time. I sat in the house by myself, watching TV. We drifted farther and farther apart and I became more and more morose. I kept telling myself I'll be pregnant soon and we'll be a normal family. I was tired of being alone. I wanted a baby. I needed a baby. I needed a baby I could love without any reservations, to have unequivocal love from, someone I could protect and create a wonderful world for, someone through whom I could erase my childhood by creating a positive for every negative that had hit me. I idealized motherhood and had this paralyzing mantra marching through my head that I wouldn't be complete until I had a baby. I had no right on this earth if I didn't reproduce. The cruel mental manipulation I subjected myself to didn't seem to have an endpoint. The thought of having a child took over. The more I focused on it, the farther away it seemed to get. Ricky went on more deployments; we fought more and spent less time doing what makes babies. The stress got worse and the mantra got louder. I was worthless. I shouldn't be taking up space on the earth. I failed as a woman. What good was I? What good could I do to balance the deficit? I would leave without producing a grandchild for my parents, and more importantly, a child for my husband. I was a worthless, worthless female.

The Lord really does know what's best for us. Had a child been born unto me at that point, it would have had a dysfunctional mother who was trying to live through her child. And there would have been so much pressure on the child to be perfect, because my whole ego would have been based on their success and failure.

Somewhere in the middle of Ricky's and my ten-year marriage, my father stopped drinking and I started to learn who he was. I had to choose to forgive. The most enlightening thing to learn in life is that you don't forgive for the other person. It really doesn't have that much to do with the other person. Forgiveness is for you. It is you choosing to release your pain and your anger and move on. You cannot move on if you always give prominence to an act someone else performed. I chose to give my father another chance. But it was so hard to get past my rearing to accept this man as my father and to give him the status of "dad." I watched the man I loved with all my heart immerge from his studded chrysalis, raw and vulnerable and open. I watched him slowly take on a different persona, one that actually laughed and smiled and said nice things. I watched him start to learn how to be happy. The main gift my father gave me when he chose sobriety was to see that you could change your path. And the seed of change was planted inside me.

Not long after my dad stopped drinking, I called Ricky over the ship-to-shore radio when he was on the USS *America* in the Indian Ocean, in the middle of ops. I told him my youngest brother, Jimmy, had died on a motorcycle, drunk.

Jimmy, my troubled, extremely handsome brother, addicted to cocaine, angry at everyone and everything, had died. End of story. No chance for redemption, no chance for mending the past, no chance to escape his childhood and be happy. Twenty and dead.

Ricky went and talked to whoever ruled the roost then, and a couple of days later he was home in California with me. But I didn't want his comfort; more telling is that I didn't need it. He tried, Lord love him, to be the good and supportive husband. I just didn't let him. I stood on my own in my grief, afraid if I bent at all I'd shatter like a crystal glass dropped on tile. It never went back together for Ricky and me after that. We never could find our way to laughter and fun again. I paint this picture of life with Ricky of misery. It wasn't miserable. It just wasn't happy

My cousins popped out babies with no issues. The wind blew up their skirts and they were pregnant. My friends were pregnant and going down and getting abortions. And no one seemed to be having their unwanted babies and giving them up for adoption. I watched every other woman's world turn. Mine was frozen and stuck

Eventually, Ricky and I moved back to California and divorced. I was crushed, yet another failure. We had nothing to hold us together and I had no idea my feelings had already changed long before we fell apart. I didn't want a divorce, because it was an admittance of failure, not because I was still head over heels for Ricky. I knew that the true reason Ricky left me was because I couldn't get pregnant. He wanted that family and that infernal clock was ticking. When I was thirty, it was pretty obvious that I was barren. Ricky walked. He went immediately (like, the same day) into another woman's arms and bed. She was pregnant in a month. He replaced me without ever looking back. He even went so far as to move her into the same apartment building we had been so happy in when we were first married.

And there it was, the utter and complete failure of my life. No husband, no children, no house, no job (I quit in the middle of all of the ensuing drama). I was an empty slate. I had no commitments to anything. I no longer felt like I had to hide my humanity. You could take me or leave me. I was who I was and I wasn't going to try to be someone else any longer. I took stock of myself, the good and the bad. I made a mental tally sheet. I was funny when I wanted to be, I was creative, disorganized, an emotional creature, passionate, whimsical, reckless, smart, could be melodramatic, flaky, dependable.

I found a job as a florist, something that I loved. The beauty of the flowers started to give me back my smiles. I made new friends. I was good at the flowers. My new life had really begun. I still was stumbling around, but I was walking taller, I was gaining momentum, and I was gaining self-love and appreciation. So I failed at the wife thing. I succeeded in other things. I was starting to see a balance in life. When something is lost, the scale is askew and something else must be gained.

As I learned a new life and a new me, I also learned a new God. I was having small conversations with God all the time. Any moment that was quiet, I had a running conversation with the Lord in my head—simple things like wondering why he created the color blue. Why in his creation there had to be an explanation of blue, why the world separated God and science from that explanation.

I started hanging out at a local pub, selling my paintings to the patrons, using the people there as subjects, doing portraits of the couples hiding in deep corners, a blue haze of cigarette smoke hiding them in the shadows, or the pool players leaning on their sticks and wobbling in their drink.

In walked this guy, no smile, no game, sitting down and watching football with his buddy. He was tall, dark-haired, intelligent-looking, and serious. I tried flirting; no response. I tried being coquettish; no response. I gave up and started drawing. Suddenly, there he was, looking at what I was doing, curious about this woman sitting in a bar, drawing and selling her work to the people there. He sat down and started talking, and I fell in love at that moment. One date, one kiss, and it was one life for the two of us.

As things progressed, I knew I had to tell him I was barren. I thought he'd leave at that moment. I thought it would be the final scene. Mike looked at me, took my face in his hands, and said that was OK, he'd be a terrible dad. I cried and thanked the Lord for sending me this man.

I thought I would be OK after getting married to a completely different type of man, a cerebral man, quiet and introverted, the diametric opposite of my first husband. I had told Mike about being barren. I had confessed and convinced him that I was not able to get pregnant, but that drive for a child became dominant once again. A sadness settled and wouldn't lift. Although I knew Mike didn't really want kids, I needed to give one last-ditch effort, so at thirty-five we started at the fertility clinic. He wanted me to be happy, so he jumped in completely. We did every embarrassing thing asked of us. I lost seventy-five pounds. Mike switched from briefs to boxers. We made love and then went immediately to the doctor's for tests. We made love on a time schedule, in required positions, did all the perfunctory sex that was required. I took the hormones, did the surgeries, was an excellent patient who did *everything* the doctor told me to. After months and month and months of this process, the doctor said our chances of conceiving were very minimal and that he strongly recommended that we start adoption proceedings before another year went by; that we would probably never produce a child on our own and to accept it and give up. I stopped treatment, started mourning, and fell into a depression.

At this time I worked at Los Altos School District and looked out the window at all the harried parents dropping their children off at daycare, feeling sad that these parents didn't seem to realize what a precious time it was in their lives. They were irritated, the kids were crying, all their days starting off in chaos. "My kids will be raised by me." "It's not worth the extra money." Oh, I was such a good mom before I had kids ☺

One day Ricky called my mother and asked her to be the grandmother to his and Barbara's child. Now, my mother's only chance to be a grandmother was through my ex-husband and my replacement. I was crushed. I was devastated. I wanted a child so badly. I admit that when I was younger I was way too damaged to be a good mother. But now I was tempered, like strong steel. I had forgiven myself my past and moved on. But now Ricky's second wife would give my mother her grandchild. My mother refused Ricky's request. I was so low. The drive for a child blinded me to the good in my life. All I could see was my failure. My poor husband saw me retreating farther and farther. I was now utterly broken. I couldn't have a child and I couldn't escape my desire for a child. I was ready to be a good parent and give everything to the child and not be looking for what the child could give to me. I had grown up. But it was never to be.

I drove out to the beach one night and just sat on a cliff, watching the waves pound. With tears rolling down my face, for the first time

I admitted my helplessness. I couldn't fix this. I couldn't force my body to work like it was supposed to. I also couldn't go on wanting a child so desperately. I did not cry out, but I whimpered like a wounded animal to my Lord, to the one I carried in my heart and spoke to in quiet moments, the one I posed weird questions to, like why he created a platypus. I wasn't trying to wheedle him; I wasn't trying to bend him to my wanting. I wanted to give up. I needed a parent; I needed my God. I needed to finally trust my God to help. In that moment I gave my pain to him because I couldn't walk with it anymore. I asked God very earnestly to either grace me with a child or take away the desire to have one. I stared at the ocean for a long time, the pounding waves seemingly pounding out the pain and filling the void with a peace I'd never known. I knew my prayer had been heard. I was at peace with being barren. The obsession with the idea of motherhood had left me. Of course I still desired a child, but suddenly I was reconciled. I'd carried the guilt of being barren since I was nineteen. I was now thirty-six, and finally I didn't have this crushing weight on my spirit.

Two months after stopping fertility treatments, I missed my period. No biggie, but I couldn't stay awake; there was this feeling of invasion. I went down and bought a pregnancy test. It came with two sticks. I psyched myself up for the letdown of seeing no pink line. I went in and did what I needed to do, capped the stick, and waited. In just a couple of minutes a line started to appear. It wasn't butterflies in my stomach, it was pterodactyls waiting for the full five minutes. And there it was, a beautiful, terrifying pink line. The tears rolled down my face. I got out the other stick, knowing this one must be defective. I have no idea how I forced out more pee, but I did. I waited. Those pterodactyls had doubled in number and grown in size twofold since five minutes prior. I waited the full five before looking again. It was pink. I started crying and couldn't stop. I shook like I was standing on a vibrating machine. The next week, the doctor ordered an ultrasound. I was seven weeks pregnant, which was about the same time I'd gone to the beach and given everything over to God.

My miracle child, Michael, was born healthy and beautiful. He was a perfect child, ten toes, ten fingers—a perfect creation of God.

A year after having Michael, we were playing in the backyard. He was crawling through his plastic balls, throwing them at the cat, who would bat them around. I was thinking how sad it was that Michael would be raised as an only child. I said a simple prayer while I watched my beautiful child play in the winter sun, asking the Lord for one more blessing, one more child for my child to have a sibling. The prayer wasn't said for me. It was said for Michael. The next month I was blessed with one more miracle at thirty-seven. I became pregnant with Matthew.

I learned without a doubt to pray without a doubt, to know that the Lord is there and to trust him to know what you need, and more importantly, when you need it. I would have been a terrible mother had I become pregnant when I was with Ricky. I needed to find stability within myself. I was blessed with a husband who loved me, who allowed me to be who I am. I grew within that relationship and put to rest my demons. I didn't need them to protect me any longer. I didn't need to wear a suit of armor. Now I had a family based on love and respect. I had a husband who supplicated himself to the Lord and who was head of this family. I had a home and I had my two miracle babies. God is good!

One more note: because of my kids, I got involved with the school. Frances Dampier was principal at Bishop, where my children attended. Someone, I have no idea who, had told her about my artistic abilities. She then asked me to paint a mural, which I did. And that one request launched an entire world for me. I now work steadily teaching art privately, doing murals and portraits professionally, and working steadily at something that allows me to be home with my kids, do what I was meant to do with my natural abilities, and all this because of a prayer on a beach a long time ago.

Chapter 6

How to Begin Writing Your Own Journal

Journaling is a unique way of expressing how miracles blossom in your life and how the Holy Spirit led you to all of your incredible miracles. It is not only therapeutic but also spiritually invigorating. T. D. Jakes once said, **"Keep journaling throughout your life. Record the events of your life, the revelations God gives you, and every way God shepherds you into new phases and opportunities."** I totally agree with his incredible insight. In this chapter, I will provide an actual event to guide you as you begin your own twenty-one-day journal. At the end of the twenty-one days, I guarantee you will become more in tune to God's interventions in your daily life. Your spirit will be rejuvenated! Let's begin.

𝒟𝒶𝓎 1: Today (insert month, day, year), I'm going to enjoy God's kisses, for they invoke joy to my soul and remind me that God loves and cares for me. I will listen for the "God Whispers" from the Holy Spirit, for he will lead me to do what is right and just. This journal entry is a testimony to God of the miracle he blessed me with on this glorious day.

𝒮𝑒𝓉 𝒾𝓉 𝓊𝓅: Explain where you were when the event happened and who was with you unless you were alone.

Friday morning, January 18, 2013. I was alone.

𝒯𝑒𝓁𝓁 𝓉𝒽𝑒 𝓂𝒾𝓇𝒶𝒸𝓁𝑒:

Today, I had a follow-up pap test appointment at Kaiser Permanente. Six months earlier, at a routine appointment the gynecologist had noticed some abnormities in the test result sample. She had set up a return appointment for today to recheck me as a precautionary measure. I wasn't really worried, because I had never had an abnormal pap test, nor did I feel any different healthwise. Usually, I pray to God to take away any harmful health issues before going in and today was no exception. Gathering up my appointment card and my purse, I hastily headed for my car. It was 10:15, so I had plenty of time to get to my 10:30 appointment because Kaiser was only ten minutes away.

As usual, I grabbed my keychain and pushed down on the car remote, expecting to hear the unlocking sound of the car door. No sound came. I pushed every button on the car remote but there was no sound at all. Suddenly, I remembered the old-fashioned way of entering the car, so I put the key in the car door. Aha, I thought, silly me. Now I'm on my way! I put the key in the ignition but there was not even a simple turning over of the engine—dead silence. Thoughts swirled through my head of what next steps to do. I looked up at the sky and said, "Lord, this is not one of my miracles. What should I do?" In an instant, the Holy Spirit told me to call Tracy Toyota. I thought to myself, why am I calling Toyota and not Geico, my car insurance company? But the Holy Spirit led me back into the house and I dialed Toyota's service department. The receptionist answered and I asked for the service department. She transferred the call immediately. I didn't know exactly why I was calling but I felt assured the Holy Spirit knew the reason. Not soon after, the phone rang and rang but nobody answered. I looked at the clock; it was 10:35. Uh-oh, I knew I was late for the appointment. Wondering what to do next, the Holy Spirit led me to call Kaiser to tell them of my dilemma. The nurse asked me if I wanted to cancel and reschedule. I asked if there was a later appointment time and she said no, but to my surprise she said I could come in and wait and if they could they would slip me in between appointments. What? I had been a member for forty years and no one had told me that. So I said I'd come over as soon as I could. She reminded me that it might be a long wait but I didn't care at that point.

Settling down, I decided that I'd better called Geico and picked up the phone to dial them, but the Holy Spirit turned my sight to the phone number I had written down for Tracy Toyota instead. Instantly, I dialed their number, thinking why am I doing this again. The receptionist answered again, but this time I blurted out about my car problems and my doctor's appointment and somehow I guess she felt sympathy for me. She instantly told me to wait until she got back. She was actually going to walk over to the service department to see if she could find a service attendant. When she returned to the phone, she assured me that she had found someone who could assist me. Wow, was I surprised! The service attendant answered and I blurted out my entire predicament, the car not starting and the doctor's appointment. He said it sounded like my car's battery was the issue. I told him that the car was only four years old. He assured me that it was either the battery or an alternator problem and suggested I call my insurance company. He asked if I had car insurance. I told him I did and was about to hang up when he said, "Wait, where do you live?" I told him my address, and to my amazement he replied, "I'll come over there in about fifteen minutes and bring my jumper equipment. Is that too long?" "Shucks no." I was thinking, whoever heard of a mechanic coming to your house? Perfectly stunned, I told him that I would be waiting for him.

Fifteen minutes later, the service attendant arrived with his jumper machine and the car started up immediately. He advised me to drive on the freeway first to get the juices flowing again. He surprisingly told me his schedule for the whole day and said if I needed him again to call him. Then he reached in his pocket and pulled out his business card and handed it to me. As he was getting in his car, I glanced down at the business card: Director of Fixed Operations/Tracy Toyota. My eyes welled up and I beckoned for him to roll down his window. I said, "Thank you so much for taking the time from your busy schedule to take care of me. You must be my guardian angel." A wide grin crossed his face and he said, "No problem, ma'am, anytime. Call me if you need me today."

Certain that God had intervened and performed a great miracle, I drove the long way to Kaiser and went straight to my gynecologist's office. I began my appointment with the usual filling out of paperwork and the nurse ushering me to take my blood pressure before seeing my doctor. When she took my blood pressure, I could tell something was wrong, because she immediately stammered that she needed to take it a second time. I asked if something was wrong with the first test. She didn't answer, so I started telling her about my car problems earlier. That seemed to relieve her fears, so she took me into the doctor's office.

The doctor asked me about my blood pressure medication and I assured her that I was taking it daily. She said that she still wanted me to take another test after her pelvic examination. She proceeded to do her pelvic exam and breast exam. She assured me that the pap test was probably nothing to worry about and advised that I would get results in two to three weeks. After the consultation, the doctor asked me to retake the blood pressure test with the nurse before leaving. When I took the test again, the nurse's eyes got large and she went to get her supervisor. I knew this wasn't a good sign. When the supervisor came and took the test again, she immediately responded that we were going to have to go over to the medical department and meet with a doctor. Now I knew this was serious, so I told her that I wanted to know right then and there what my blood pressure reading was! She told me that it was 186 over 103. I knew the normal reading was around 125 over 80. To calm their fears, I told them that I had been taking a green bean herbal supplement but I researched it and found no side effects. That didn't seem to calm them down one bit, so they ushered me over to the medical department's waiting room. Meanwhile, I was beginning to understand the seriousness of this problem. I called my own doctor, who was at another Kaiser facility, and told his nurse what had occurred. She told me that my doctor would call me in fifteen minutes. Meanwhile, the supervisor nurse took me into the doctor's office, where they were trying to decide whether to put me on some medication to bring down my pressure or send me to the hospital. Luckily, my own physician called and we decided to increase my medication over a period of a few weeks and to take a blood test to see if the medication was working effectively. He said I was lucky that I happened to be in the doctor's office when my blood pressure skyrocketed because it was at stroke level.

Recognize the miracle:

I thought to myself that was not luck or coincidence. The entire day was a miracle. I didn't know it at the time, but I was lucky the car didn't start because it made me late for my appointment. The nurse said there had been a lot of people before I came, but I didn't get there until right before lunch, so the office had cleared out and they had no one there but me to look after when I arrived.

The mechanic who helped me was God's angel, because if I had called Geico, it would have taken one or more hours for them to get to me, and most of all, I had no idea that my blood pressure was so high. It was through God's miracle that on this specific day he made sure that I was in the right place with medical doctors and services readily available for me, a child of the most high. Wow! How mind-blowing is this miracle? My God is indeed all powerful and all knowing.

Go tell it:

God wants us to go tell someone when he blesses us. The mere excitement in our voices when we blurt out the miracle can convince another person. Sometimes they will tell you a similar story, which confirms to them that their story is credible and indeed a miracle from God. Immediately, I called my sons to tell them what had occurred. They were very concerned but no match for my rambling on and on about God's miracle in the whole process. Later, I told every person I spoke with on the phone who would listen.

Praise God:

I thanked God for letting me be the recipient of such a glorious gift. As always, I usually get teary-eyed when God blesses me in such a magnificent way. Just the mere thought of what he did on one magnificent day in my life makes me so proud to be one of God's disciples. I thanked him for giving me the gift of the Holy Spirit within me to abide and guide me in my daily life's journeys.

Write it down:

Keeping a journal for me is a way to affirm God's miracles, but also a way of having a record to look back on when things get tough and when troubled times occur in life. Sometimes we are burdened with things that seem too heavy to bear alone and we can turn back a few pages in our journal and know that God was there with us the whole time. My favorite poem is "Footprints." Sometimes I read it over and over. The words are so comforting. When we think we are suffering all alone, God's words echo to me, "My precious child, I love you and would never leave you. During your times of trial and suffering, when you see only one set of footprints, it was then that I *carried you.*"

Chapter 7

Miracles Blossom from the Spirit within Journal

JOURNAL

_____

NAME

Miracle Journal Entry for the Spirit Within

Day 1: Today ————————, I'm going to enjoy God's kisses for they invoke joy to my soul and remind me that God loves and cares for me. I will listen for the "God Whispers" from the Holy Spirit for he will lead me to do what is right and just. This journal entry is a testimony to God of the miracle he blessed me with on this glorious day.

Set it Up: Explain where you were when the event happened and who was with you unless you were alone.

Set	It	Up

_____

_____

Tell the Miracles: Be precise, concise and give sequential details.

Tell	The	Miracles

_____

_____

_____

_____

_____

_____

_____

_____

_____

_____

<u>Recognize the Miracle</u>: Did you know right away that you were experiencing a miracle?

Recognize	>	The	>	Miracles

_____

_____

<u>Go tell it</u>: Make sure you tell someone about your miracle while your joy is infectious.

Go	>	Tell	>	It

_____

_____

<u>Praise God</u>: Thank God Almighty for blessing you with this glorious gift.

Praise	>	God	>	Almighty

_____

_____

Write it Down: Keep a daily diary each day no matter how small the miracle. If you woke up today, start writing that as your first miracle of the day.

Write	It	Down

_____

_____

_____

_____

_____

_____

"Every hour God looks after you."
2: Thessalonians 3:3

"Every minute God cares for you."
1 Peter 5:7

Miracle Journal Entry for the Spirit Within

Day 2: Today ——————————, I'm going to enjoy God's kisses for they invoke joy to my soul and remind me that God loves and cares for me. I will listen for the "God Whispers" from the Holy Spirit for he will lead me to do what is right and just. This journal entry is a testimony to God of the miracle he blessed me with on this glorious day.

<u>Set it Up</u>: Explain where you were when the event happened and who was with you unless you were alone.

Set ⟩ It ⟩ Up

_____

_____

Tell the Miracles: Be precise, concise and give sequential details.

Tell	The	Miracles

_____

_____

_____

_____

_____

_____

_____

_____

_____

Recognize the Miracle: Did you know right away that you were experiencing a miracle?

Recognize	The	Miracles

Go tell it: Make sure you tell someone about your miracle while your joy is infectious.

Go	Tell	It

Praise God: Thank God Almighty for blessing you with this glorious gift.

Praise	God	Almighty

Write it Down: Keep a daily diary each day no matter how small the miracle. If you woke up today, start writing that as your first miracle of the day.

Write	It	Down

_____

_____

_____

_____

_____

_____

"Every hour God looks after you."
2: Thessalonians 3:3

"Every minute God cares for you."
1 Peter 5:7

Miracle Journal Entry for the Spirit Within

Day 3: Today ——————————, I'm going to enjoy God's kisses for they invoke joy to my soul and remind me that God loves and cares for me. I will listen for the "God Whispers" from the Holy Spirit for he will lead me to do what is right and just. This journal entry is a testimony to God of the miracle he blessed me with on this glorious day.

Set it Up: Explain where you were when the event happened and who was with you unless you were alone.

Set	It	Up

_____

_____

Tell the Miracles: Be precise, concise and give sequential details.

Tell	The	Miracles

_____

_____

_____

_____

_____

_____

_____

_____

_____

_____

Recognize the Miracle: Did you know right away that you were experiencing a miracle?

Recognize	The	Miracles

Go tell it: Make sure you tell someone about your miracle while your joy is infectious.

Go	Tell	It

Praise God: Thank God Almighty for blessing you with this glorious gift.

Praise	God	Almighty

Write it Down: Keep a daily diary each day no matter how small the miracle. If you woke up today, start writing that as your first miracle of the day.

Write ⟩ It ⟩ Down

_____

_____

_____

_____

_____

_____

"Every hour God looks after you."
2: Thessalonians 3:3

"Every minute God cares for you."
1 Peter 5:7

Miracle Journal Entry for the Spirit Within

Day 4: Today ———————————, I'm going to enjoy God's kisses for they invoke joy to my soul and remind me that God loves and cares for me. I will listen for the "God Whispers" from the Holy Spirit for he will lead me to do what is right and just. This journal entry is a testimony to God of the miracle he blessed me with on this glorious day.

Set it Up: Explain where you were when the event happened and who was with you unless you were alone.

Set	It	Up

_____

_____

Tell the Miracles: Be precise, concise and give sequential details.

> Tell > The > Miracles

_____

_____

_____

_____

_____

_____

_____

_____

_____

<u>Recognize the Miracle:</u> Did you know right away that you were experiencing a miracle?

Recognize	The	Miracles

_____

_____

<u>Go tell it:</u> Make sure you tell someone about your miracle while your joy is infectious.

Go	Tell	It

_____

_____

<u>Praise God:</u> Thank God Almighty for blessing you with this glorious gift.

Praise	God	Almighty

_____

_____

<u>Write it Down:</u> Keep a daily diary each day no matter how small the miracle. If you woke up today, start writing that as your first miracle of the day.

> Write ▷ It ▷ Down

_____

_____

_____

_____

_____

_____

"Every hour God looks after you."
2: Thessalonians 3:3

"Every minute God cares for you."
1 Peter 5:7

Miracle Journal Entry for the Spirit Within

Day 5: Today _____, I'm going to enjoy God's kisses for they invoke joy to my soul and remind me that God loves and cares for me. I will listen for the "God Whispers" from the Holy Spirit for he will lead me to do what is right and just. This journal entry is a testimony to God of the miracle he blessed me with on this glorious day.

Set it Up: Explain where you were when the event happened and who was with you unless you were alone.

Set	It	Up

_____

_____

Tell the Miracles: Be precise, concise and give sequential details.

Tell	The	Miracles

_____

_____

_____

_____

_____

_____

_____

_____

_____

_____

Recognize the Miracle: Did you know right away that you were experiencing a miracle?

Recognize	The	Miracles

_____

_____

Go tell it: Make sure you tell someone about your miracle while your joy is infectious.

Go	Tell	It

_____

_____

Praise God: Thank God Almighty for blessing you with this glorious gift.

Praise	God	Almighty

_____

_____

Write it Down: Keep a daily diary each day no matter how small the miracle. If you woke up today, start writing that as your first miracle of the day.

Write	It	Down

_____

_____

_____

_____

_____

_____

"Every hour God looks after you."
2: Thessalonians 3:3

"Every minute God cares for you."
1 Peter 5:7

Miracle Journal Entry for the Spirit Within

Day 6: Today _____, I'm going to enjoy God's kisses for they invoke joy to my soul and remind me that God loves and cares for me. I will listen for the "God Whispers" from the Holy Spirit for he will lead me to do what is right and just. This journal entry is a testimony to God of the miracle he blessed me with on this glorious day.

Set it Up: Explain where you were when the event happened and who was with you unless you were alone.

Set	It	Up

_____

_____

Tell the Miracles: Be precise, concise and give sequential details.

Tell	The	Miracles

_____

_____

_____

_____

_____

_____

_____

_____

_____

Recognize the Miracle: Did you know right away that you were experiencing a miracle?

Recognize	The	Miracles

_____

_____

Go tell it: Make sure you tell someone about your miracle while your joy is infectious.

Go	Tell	It

_____

_____

Praise God: Thank God Almighty for blessing you with this glorious gift.

Praise	God	Almighty

_____

_____

Write it Down: Keep a daily diary each day no matter how small the miracle. If you woke up today, start writing that as your first miracle of the day.

Write	It	Down

_____

_____

_____

_____

_____

_____

"Every hour God looks after you."
2: Thessalonians 3:3

"Every minute God cares for you."
1 Peter 5:7

Miracle Journal Entry for the Spirit Within

Day 7: Today ——————————, I'm going to enjoy God's kisses for they invoke joy to my soul and remind me that God loves and cares for me. I will listen for the "God Whispers" from the Holy Spirit for he will lead me to do what is right and just. This journal entry is a testimony to God of the miracle he blessed me with on this glorious day.

Set it Up: Explain where you were when the event happened and who was with you unless you were alone.

Set	It	Up

_____

_____

Tell the Miracles: Be precise, concise and give sequential details.

Tell	The	Miracles

_____

_____

_____

_____

_____

_____

_____

_____

_____

_____

Recognize the Miracle: Did you know right away that you were experiencing a miracle?

Recognize	The	Miracles

Go tell it: Make sure you tell someone about your miracle while your joy is infectious.

Go	Tell	It

Praise God: Thank God Almighty for blessing you with this glorious gift.

Praise	God	Almighty

<u>Write it Down</u>: Keep a daily diary each day no matter how small the miracle. If you woke up today, start writing that as your first miracle of the day.

Write	It	Down

_____

_____

_____

_____

_____

_____

"Every hour God looks after you."
2: Thessalonians 3:3

"Every minute God cares for you."
1 Peter 5:7

Miracle Journal Entry for the Spirit Within

Day 8: Today ———————, I'm going to enjoy God's kisses for they invoke joy to my soul and remind me that God loves and cares for me. I will listen for the "God Whispers" from the Holy Spirit for he will lead me to do what is right and just. This journal entry is a testimony to God of the miracle he blessed me with on this glorious day.

Set it Up: Explain where you were when the event happened and who was with you unless you were alone.

Set	It	Up

_____

_____

Tell the Miracles: Be precise, concise and give sequential details.

Tell	The	Miracles

_____

_____

_____

_____

_____

_____

_____

_____

_____

_____

Recognize the Miracle: Did you know right away that you were experiencing a miracle?

Recognize	The	Miracles

_____

_____

Go tell it: Make sure you tell someone about your miracle while your joy is infectious.

Go	Tell	It

_____

_____

Praise God: Thank God Almighty for blessing you with this glorious gift.

Praise	God	Almighty

_____

_____

Write it Down: Keep a daily diary each day no matter how small the miracle. If you woke up today, start writing that as your first miracle of the day.

Write	It	Down

_____

_____

_____

_____

_____

_____

"Every hour God looks after you."
2: Thessalonians 3:3

"Every minute God cares for you."
1 Peter 5:7

Miracle Journal Entry for the Spirit Within

Day 9: Today ————————————, I'm going to enjoy God's kisses for they invoke joy to my soul and remind me that God loves and cares for me. I will listen for the "God Whispers" from the Holy Spirit for he will lead me to do what is right and just. This journal entry is a testimony to God of the miracle he blessed me with on this glorious day.

Set it Up: Explain where you were when the event happened and who was with you unless you were alone.

Set	It	Up

_____

_____

Tell the Miracles: Be precise, concise and give sequential details.

Tell	The	Miracles

_____
_____
_____
_____
_____
_____
_____
_____
_____
_____

Recognize the Miracle: Did you know right away that you were experiencing a miracle?

Recognize	The	Miracles

_____

_____

Go tell it: Make sure you tell someone about your miracle while your joy is infectious.

Go	Tell	It

_____

_____

Praise God: Thank God Almighty for blessing you with this glorious gift.

Praise	God	Almighty

_____

_____

Write it Down: Keep a daily diary each day no matter how small the miracle. If you woke up today, start writing that as your first miracle of the day.

Write ▷ It ▷ Down

_____

_____

_____

_____

_____

_____

"Every hour God looks after you."
2: Thessalonians 3:3

"Every minute God cares for you."
1 Peter 5:7

Miracle Journal Entry for the Spirit Within

Day 10: Today _____, I'm going to enjoy God's kisses for they invoke joy to my soul and remind me that God loves and cares for me. I will listen for the "God Whispers" from the Holy Spirit for he will lead me to do what is right and just. This journal entry is a testimony to God of the miracle he blessed me with on this glorious day.

Set it Up: Explain where you were when the event happened and who was with you unless you were alone.

Set	It	Up

_____

_____

Tell the Miracles: Be precise, concise and give sequential details.

Tell	The	Miracles

_____

_____

_____

_____

_____

_____

_____

_____

_____

Recognize the Miracle: Did you know right away that you were experiencing a miracle?

Recognize	The	Miracles

Go tell it: Make sure you tell someone about your miracle while your joy is infectious.

Go	Tell	It

Praise God: Thank God Almighty for blessing you with this glorious gift.

Praise	God	Almighty

Write it Down: Keep a daily diary each day no matter how small the miracle. If you woke up today, start writing that as your first miracle of the day.

Write It Down

_____

_____

_____

_____

_____

_____

"Every hour God looks after you."
2: Thessalonians 3:3

"Every minute God cares for you."
1 Peter 5:7

Miracle Journal Entry for the Spirit Within

Day 11: Today ——————————, I'm going to enjoy God's kisses for they invoke joy to my soul and remind me that God loves and cares for me. I will listen for the "God Whispers" from the Holy Spirit for he will lead me to do what is right and just. This journal entry is a testimony to God of the miracle he blessed me with on this glorious day.

Set it Up: Explain where you were when the event happened and who was with you unless you were alone.

Set	It	Up

_____

_____

__Tell the Miracles:__ Be precise, concise and give sequential details.

Tell	The	Miracles

_____

_____

_____

_____

_____

_____

_____

_____

_____

_____

Recognize the Miracle: Did you know right away that you were experiencing a miracle?

Recognize	The	Miracles

_____

_____

Go tell it: Make sure you tell someone about your miracle while your joy is infectious.

Go	Tell	It

_____

_____

Praise God: Thank God Almighty for blessing you with this glorious gift.

Praise	God	Almighty

_____

_____

<u>__Write it Down:__</u> Keep a daily diary each day no matter how small the miracle. If you woke up today, start writing that as your first miracle of the day.

Write	It	Down

_____

_____

_____

_____

_____

_____

_____

_____

"Every hour God looks after you."
2: Thessalonians 3:3

"Every minute God cares for you."
1 Peter 5:7

Miracle Journal Entry for the Spirit Within

Day 12: Today ─────────────, I'm going to enjoy God's kisses for they invoke joy to my soul and remind me that God loves and cares for me. I will listen for the "God Whispers" from the Holy Spirit for he will lead me to do what is right and just. This journal entry is a testimony to God of the miracle he blessed me with on this glorious day.

Set it Up: Explain where you were when the event happened and who was with you unless you were alone.

Set	It	Up

_____

_____

Tell the Miracles: Be precise, concise and give sequential details.

Tell	The	Miracles

_____

_____

_____

_____

_____

_____

_____

_____

_____

<u>Recognize the Miracle</u>: Did you know right away that you were experiencing a miracle?

Recognize	The	Miracles

_____

_____

<u>Go tell it</u>: Make sure you tell someone about your miracle while your joy is infectious.

Go	Tell	It

_____

_____

<u>Praise God</u>: Thank God Almighty for blessing you with this glorious gift.

Praise	God	Almighty

_____

_____

Write it Down: Keep a daily diary each day no matter how small the miracle. If you woke up today, start writing that as your first miracle of the day.

Write > It > Down

_____

_____

_____

_____

_____

_____

"Every hour God looks after you."
2: Thessalonians 3:3

"Every minute God cares for you."
1 Peter 5:7

Miracle Journal Entry for the Spirit Within

Day 13: Today _____, I'm going to enjoy God's kisses for they invoke joy to my soul and remind me that God loves and cares for me. I will listen for the "God Whispers" from the Holy Spirit for he will lead me to do what is right and just. This journal entry is a testimony to God of the miracle he blessed me with on this glorious day.

Set it Up: Explain where you were when the event happened and who was with you unless you were alone.

Set ▷ It ▷ Up

_____

_____

Tell the Miracles: Be precise, concise and give sequential details.

Tell	The	Miracles

_____

_____

_____

_____

_____

_____

_____

_____

_____

_____

Recognize the Miracle: Did you know right away that you were experiencing a miracle?

Recognize	The	Miracles

_____

_____

Go tell it: Make sure you tell someone about your miracle while your joy is infectious.

Go	Tell	It

_____

_____

Praise God: Thank God Almighty for blessing you with this glorious gift.

Praise	God	Almighty

_____

_____

Write it Down: Keep a daily diary each day no matter how small the miracle. If you woke up today, start writing that as your first miracle of the day.

Write	It	Down

_____

_____

_____

_____

_____

_____

"*Every hour God looks after you.*"
2: Thessalonians 3:3

"*Every minute God cares for you.*"
1 Peter 5:7

Miracle Journal Entry for the Spirit Within

Day 14: Today ——————————, I'm going to enjoy God's kisses for they invoke joy to my soul and remind me that God loves and cares for me. I will listen for the "God Whispers" from the Holy Spirit for he will lead me to do what is right and just. This journal entry is a testimony to God of the miracle he blessed me with on this glorious day.

<u>Set it Up</u>: Explain where you were when the event happened and who was with you unless you were alone.

Set	It	Up

———————————————————————

———————————————————————

Tell the Miracles: Be precise, concise and give sequential details.

> Tell ⟩ The ⟩ Miracles

_____

_____

_____

_____

_____

_____

_____

_____

_____

Recognize the Miracle: Did you know right away that you were experiencing a miracle?

Recognize	The	Miracles

_____

_____

Go tell it: Make sure you tell someone about your miracle while your joy is infectious.

Go	Tell	It

_____

_____

Praise God: Thank God Almighty for blessing you with this glorious gift.

Praise	God	Almighty

_____

_____

Write it Down: Keep a daily diary each day no matter how small the miracle. If you woke up today, start writing that as your first miracle of the day.

> Write > It > Down

_____

_____

_____

_____

_____

_____

"Every hour God looks after you."
2: Thessalonians 3:3

"Every minute God cares for you."
1 Peter 5:7

Miracle Journal Entry for the Spirit Within

Day 15: Today ———————————, I'm going to enjoy God's kisses for they invoke joy to my soul and remind me that God loves and cares for me. I will listen for the "God Whispers" from the Holy Spirit for he will lead me to do what is right and just. This journal entry is a testimony to God of the miracle he blessed me with on this glorious day.

Set it Up: Explain where you were when the event happened and who was with you unless you were alone.

Set	It	Up

_____

_____

Tell the Miracles: Be precise, concise and give sequential details.

Tell	The	Miracles

_____

_____

_____

_____

_____

_____

_____

_____

_____

Recognize the Miracle: Did you know right away that you were experiencing a miracle?

Recognize	The	Miracles

_____

_____

Go tell it: Make sure you tell someone about your miracle while your joy is infectious.

Go	Tell	It

_____

_____

Praise God: Thank God Almighty for blessing you with this glorious gift.

Praise	God	Almighty

_____

_____

<u>Write it Down:</u> Keep a daily diary each day no matter how small the miracle. If you woke up today, start writing that as your first miracle of the day.

> Write > It > Down

_____

_____

_____

_____

_____

_____

"Every hour God looks after you."
2: Thessalonians 3:3

"Every minute God cares for you."
1 Peter 5:7

Miracle Journal Entry for the Spirit Within

Day 16: Today _____, I'm going to enjoy God's kisses for they invoke joy to my soul and remind me that God loves and cares for me. I will listen for the "God Whispers" from the Holy Spirit for he will lead me to do what is right and just. This journal entry is a testimony to God of the miracle he blessed me with on this glorious day.

Set it Up: Explain where you were when the event happened and who was with you unless you were alone.

Set	It	Up

_____

_____

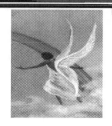

Tell the Miracles: Be precise, concise and give sequential details.

Tell	The	Miracles

_____

_____

_____

_____

_____

_____

_____

_____

_____

Recognize the Miracle: Did you know right away that you were experiencing a miracle?

Recognize	The	Miracles

_____

_____

Go tell it: Make sure you tell someone about your miracle while your joy is infectious.

Go	Tell	It

_____

_____

Praise God: Thank God Almighty for blessing you with this glorious gift.

Praise	God	Almighty

_____

_____

Write it Down: Keep a daily diary each day no matter how small the miracle. If you woke up today, start writing that as your first miracle of the day.

Write > It > Down

_____

_____

_____

_____

_____

_____

"Every hour God looks after you."
2: Thessalonians 3:3

"Every minute God cares for you."
1 Peter 5:7

172

Miracle Journal Entry for the Spirit Within

Day 17: Today _____, I'm going to enjoy God's kisses for they invoke joy to my soul and remind me that God loves and cares for me. I will listen for the "God Whispers" from the Holy Spirit for he will lead me to do what is right and just. This journal entry is a testimony to God of the miracle he blessed me with on this glorious day.

Set it Up: Explain where you were when the event happened and who was with you unless you were alone.

Set	It	Up

_____

_____

Tell the Miracles: Be precise, concise and give sequential details.

Tell	The	Miracles

_____

_____

_____

_____

_____

_____

_____

_____

_____

_____

Recognize the Miracle: Did you know right away that you were experiencing a miracle?

Recognize	The	Miracles

Go tell it: Make sure you tell someone about your miracle while your joy is infectious.

Go	Tell	It

Praise God: Thank God Almighty for blessing you with this glorious gift.

Praise	God	Almighty

Write it Down: Keep a daily diary each day no matter how small the miracle. If you woke up today, start writing that as your first miracle of the day.

> Write > It > Down

_____

_____

_____

_____

_____

_____

"Every hour God looks after you."
2: Thessalonians 3:3

"Every minute God cares for you."
1 Peter 5:7

Miracle Journal Entry for the Spirit Within

Day 18: Today _____, I'm going to enjoy God's kisses for they invoke joy to my soul and remind me that God loves and cares for me. I will listen for the "God Whispers" from the Holy Spirit for he will lead me to do what is right and just. This journal entry is a testimony to God of the miracle he blessed me with on this glorious day.

Set it Up: Explain where you were when the event happened and who was with you unless you were alone.

Set	It	Up

_____

_____

Tell the Miracles: Be precise, concise and give sequential details.

Tell	The	Miracles

_____

_____

_____

_____

_____

_____

_____

_____

_____

_____

Recognize the Miracle: Did you know right away that you were experiencing a miracle?

Recognize	The	Miracles

_____

_____

Go tell it: Make sure you tell someone about your miracle while your joy is infectious.

Go	Tell	It

_____

_____

Praise God: Thank God Almighty for blessing you with this glorious gift.

Praise	God	Almighty

_____

_____

Write it Down: Keep a daily diary each day no matter how small the miracle. If you woke up today, start writing that as your first miracle of the day.

Write > It > Down

_____

_____

_____

_____

_____

_____

"Every hour God looks after you."
2: Thessalonians 3:3

"Every minute God cares for you."
1 Peter 5:7

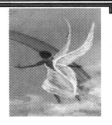

Miracle Journal Entry for the Spirit Within

Day 19: Today ———————————, I'm going to enjoy God's kisses for they invoke joy to my soul and remind me that God loves and cares for me. I will listen for the "God Whispers" from the Holy Spirit for he will lead me to do what is right and just. This journal entry is a testimony to God of the miracle he blessed me with on this glorious day.

Set it Up: Explain where you were when the event happened and who was with you unless you were alone.

Set	It	Up

———————————————————————

———————————————————————

Tell the Miracles: Be precise, concise and give sequential details.

Tell	The	Miracles

_____

_____

_____

_____

_____

_____

_____

_____

_____

_____

Recognize the Miracle: Did you know right away that you were experiencing a miracle?

Recognize	The	Miracles

_____

_____

Go tell it: Make sure you tell someone about your miracle while your joy is infectious.

Go	Tell	It

_____

_____

Praise God: Thank God Almighty for blessing you with this glorious gift.

Praise	God	Almighty

_____

_____

Write it Down: Keep a daily diary each day no matter how small the miracle. If you woke up today, start writing that as your first miracle of the day.

Write ▷ It ▷ Down

_____

_____

_____

_____

_____

_____

"Every hour God looks after you."
2: Thessalonians 3:3

"Every minute God cares for you."
1 Peter 5:7

Miracle Journal Entry for the Spirit Within

Day 20: Today _____, I'm going to enjoy God's kisses for they invoke joy to my soul and remind me that God loves and cares for me. I will listen for the "God Whispers" from the Holy Spirit for he will lead me to do what is right and just. This journal entry is a testimony to God of the miracle he blessed me with on this glorious day.

Set it Up: Explain where you were when the event happened and who was with you unless you were alone.

Set | It | Up

_____

_____

Tell the Miracles: Be precise, concise and give sequential details.

Tell	The	Miracles

_____
_____
_____
_____
_____
_____
_____
_____
_____
_____

Recognize the Miracle: Did you know right away that you were experiencing a miracle?

Recognize >	The >	Miracles >

Go tell it: Make sure you tell someone about your miracle while your joy is infectious.

Go >	Tell >	It >

Praise God: Thank God Almighty for blessing you with this glorious gift.

Praise >	God >	Almighty >

Write it Down: Keep a daily diary each day no matter how small the miracle. If you woke up today, start writing that as your first miracle of the day.

Write ▷ It ▷ Down

_____

_____

_____

_____

_____

_____

"Every hour God looks after you."
2: Thessalonians 3:3

"Every minute God cares for you."
1 Peter 5:7

Miracle Journal Entry for the Spirit Within

Day 21: Today ——————————, I'm going to enjoy God's kisses for they invoke joy to my soul and remind me that God loves and cares for me. I will listen for the "God Whispers" from the Holy Spirit for he will lead me to do what is right and just. This journal entry is a testimony to God of the miracle he blessed me with on this glorious day.

Set it Up: Explain where you were when the event happened and who was with you unless you were alone.

Set	It	Up

_____

_____

Tell the Miracles: Be precise, concise and give sequential details.

Tell	The	Miracles

_____

_____

_____

_____

_____

_____

_____

_____

_____